ZAK YNT HOS

KEFALONIA, ITHACA & L

T0243349

Travel with Marco Polo Insider Tips

INSIDER TIP
Your shortcut to a great experience

MARCO POLO TOP HIGHLIGHTS

ARGOSTOLI ⭐

Cross the world's longest stone sea bridge to get to the lively alleyways of the Mediterranean town of Argostoli.
📷 *Tip: The waves make a great backdrop for a wildly romantic portrait.*

➤ p. 66, Kefalonia

BLUE CAVES (GALAZIA SPILEA) ⭐

The Blue Caves open out into the sea through huge rocky arches. Inside, expect a spectacle of blue and turquoise hues.
📷 *Tip: The boat crew will give you a piece of white cardboard to hold on the water to capture the true blue inside the cave.*

➤ p. 47, Zakynthos

MELISSANI CAVE ⭐

Still waters run deep: take a silent boat trip into the magical light of a Kefalonia cave that was dedicated to Pan, the god of the wild, shepherds and their flocks.

➤ p. 71, Kefalonia

ASSOS ⭐

A castle, a village, a bay with a small beach: the perfect Kefalonia idyll.
📷 *Tip: From the bench on the trail up to the castle, zoom into the village below and the opposite hillside.*

➤ p. 71, Kefalonia

SHIPWRECK BEACH (NAVAGIO) ⭐

Named after a ship that ran aground here, this fabulous cove is only accessible by boat.

➤ p. 47, Zakynthos

FISKARDO
Picture-postcard scenery – arguably Kefalonia's most beautiful town, with a lovely harbour atmosphere (photo).

➤ p. 72, Kefalonia

MIRTOS BEACH
The vast beach, set between impressive cliffs, offers no distractions apart from the sound of the waves.

📷 *Tip: Capture the spectacular swell at a shutter speed of 1/500s: the ideal wallpaper for your computer!*

➤ p. 77, Kefalonia

LEFKADA TOWN
Salsa, mojitos and pastel colours – the island's capital is as cheerful as the Caribbean.

📷 *Tip: From the walls of the Agia Mavra fort, you can capture a panorama of the marina and the town.*

➤ p. 90, Lefkada

KIONI
Finally, switch off. In the most beautiful village on Ithaca, most people are on foot, and there is hardly a car in sight.

➤ p. 83, Ithaca

PORTO KATSIKI
Too beautiful to be true: a long beach backed by white cliffs. Big enough for all to find their place in the sun!

➤ p. 96, Lefkada

CONTENTS

LEFKADA

ITHACA

KEFALONIA

ZAKYNTHOS

CONTENTS

☉   Plan your visit   ♟ Eating/drinking

€–€€€   Price categories   🛍 Shopping

(*)   Premium-rate   ⏦ Going out
      phone number
                             🏖 Top beaches

(🗺 A2) Refers to the removable pull-out map
(0) Located off the map

Argostoli

BEST OF THE IONIAN ISLANDS

Set sail and explore the Ionian Islands by boat

BEST ☂

WHEN IT RAINS

ACTIVITIES TO BRIGHTEN YOUR DAY

SIMPLY DIVE IN

You don't know it's raining when you're under water. In Limni Keriou on Zakynthos you can book a short introductory dive course at one of two local *diving schools*.

➤ p. 34, Sport & activities

CLOUD LANDSCAPES

Rain showers often produce bizarre cloud formations, and a great place to watch the skies from is the *Fioro tou Levante* taverna in Ano Gerakari. Here, the whole of Zakynthos lies at your feet.

➤ p. 53, Zakynthos

MAKE POTTERY TURTLES

It could be a blessing in disguise if it rains on a Tuesday or a Saturday, when *Hanne Mi's Ceramic Art Studio* on Zakynthos is open to the public and you can try to make your own ceramic sea turtle.

➤ p. 55, Zakynthos

EXPLORE THE UNDERWORLD

In the *Drogarati Cave* (photo) on Kefalonia, water drips from the ceiling, but nobody gets wet. Over the millennia the water has formed into bizarrely shaped stalagmites and stalactites.

➤ p. 70, Kefalonia

SUPERB SHOPPING

Whether it's clothes, sunglasses, souvenirs or regional, sweet or savoury delicacies, the pedestrian zone in *Lefkada Town* is superb for shopping and browsing. And in bad weather, if you are lucky, one of the spirits shops may offer you a tasting session for free ...

➤ p. 90, Lefkada

BEST 🐷
ON A BUDGET

FOR SMALLER WALLETS

A BIG HIGHLIGHT FOR LITTLE MONEY

At the time of writing, the cheapest option for boat trips to the *Blue Caves* and *Shipwreck Beach* on Zakynthos – an absolute must-do trip – is from the lighthouse at *Cape Skinari* in the north of the island. Boats depart for the caves several times an hour, and for Shipwreck Beach several times a day.

➤ p. 47, Zakynthos

LIQUID GOLD

You can see how olive oil is made at a modern *olive press* in Lithakia on Zakynthos during the winter, and hear an explanation of the process throughout the year. Tasting is part of the experience, of course.

➤ p. 52, Zakynthos

DELICIOUS LUNCH

Every day, restaurant *To Kantoúni* on Zakynthos allows you to choose between seven dishes, freshly prepared by Sakis Zougras's mother. The restaurant is popular with local people because of the generous servings and reasonable prices.

➤ p. 55, Zakynthos

FRY YOUR OWN FRESH FISH

If you like to cook for yourself, cheap fresh fish is available in *Argostoli* (photo) on Kefalonia. Every morning, the fishermen sell their catch at the pier and the nearby market provides fresh vegetables.

➤ p. 66, Kefalonia

WINE STRAIGHT FROM THE VINYARD

The *Lefkaditiki Gi* (Lefkas Earth) *winery* hosts a small exhibition and offers guided tours of the estate, including a free tasting of their house wines without any obligation to buy. Enjoy this inviting offer!

➤ p. 94, Lefkada

BEST WITH CHILDREN

FUN FOR YOUNG & OLD

EXPLORE THE TAR PITS

At the *tar pits in Limni Keriou*, the guides prepare twigs so visitors can collect the natural tar from the spring to take home, ideally in a sealable box! Tar played a fascinating role in the island's history as it was used in centuries past to seal the hulls of ships.
➤ p. 53, Zakynthos

A FAMILY DAY OUT

Families can spend an enjoyable half day at the small *Karavomilos lake*, in the water or in hammocks and deck-chairs. The narrow pebble beach is suitable for children, the lake is sur-rounded by shady trees, there are ducks to feed and a cup of coffee to enjoy.
➤ p. 71, Kefalonia

MYTHS AT THE THEME PARK

Mythology meets animal park: you won't be bored at the *Odysseus Zoo Land* in Kefalonia. Larger-than-life heroes from Greek mythology form the backdrop for the petting zoo.
➤ p. 75, Kefalonia

HIKING WITH DONKEYS

Hiking is even more fun when donkeys walk alongside you. Those who weigh less than 55kg may ride the animals. Here, children are on top: what fun!
➤ p. 75, Kefalonia

AT THE WHEEL

The *Fantastic Park* is a permanent fair-ground at the northern end of the Odos Rizospaston in Argostoli. It is perfect for children to let off steam, take a trip in an electric jeep or "sail" remote-control boats.
➤ p. 75, Kefalonia

BEST ⚑

CLASSIC EXPERIENCES

ONLY ON THE IONIAN ISLANDS

TRADITIONAL DANCES

Folk dances can teach you about Ionian culture and allow you to get in touch with your body. Beate Knapp offers dance courses in the large courtyard of her *Beatehouses* resort in Laganas on Zakynthos.

➤ p. 59, Zakynthos

LISTEN TO KANTADES

The Zakynthians have a reputation for being the Greeks who love to sing. Everyone sings along when typical Zakynthian *kantades* are performed, as happens every evening in the *Varkarola* taverna in the island's capital, Zakynthos Town.

➤ p. 61, Zakynthos

NOSTALGIC SCENERY

Go time-travelling! After the devastating earthquake of 1953, shipping magnate George Vergottis rebuilt the neighbouring villages of *Metaxata* and *Kourkoumelta* on Kefalonia. The result were stylish settlements with villas built in typical 1950s style – they'd make great film sets!

➤ p. 68, Kefalonia

REGIONAL CUISINE

To unveil the mysteries of Ionian island cuisine, book an evening cooking course at *Chez Vassiliki* in the village of Karavados on Kefalonia. Herbs and other ingredients are gathered from the garden and then prepared and enjoyed with other international guests.

➤ p. 75, Kefalonia

FLAMINGO SAFARI

From autumn to spring, you can watch hundreds of flamingos in the shallow wetlands (photo) from the elevated position of the *Agia Mavra* fort: a sea of pink birds! Photographers will find it quite easy to get close.

➤ p. 91, Lefkada

GET TO KNOW THE IONIAN ISLANDS

The colourful coastal village of Fiskardo on Kefalonia

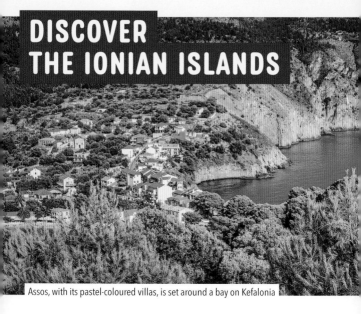

DISCOVER THE IONIAN ISLANDS

Assos, with its pastel-coloured villas, is set around a bay on Kefalonia

Boats that sail into blue grottos, white cliffs that plunge almost vertically into the sea and olive groves that sweep right up to the coast. Picturesque villages, ancient castles, bathing beaches: Zakynthos and its neighbouring islands are a real-life paradise.

MADE FOR A HOLIDAY – THE MAGICAL ISLES

Secluded coves, only accessible by boat, frame the Ionian Sea, which shimmers in myriad hues of turquoise and blue. These really are dream islands.

Off the west coast of Greece, the Ionian Islands stretch over a length of 240km. Seven of them comprise the actual political union of the Ionian Islands (*Eptanisa* in Greek): Corfu in the north, its small neighbour Paxos, Ithaca, with Kefalonia to its south, followed by Zakynthos further south. Lefkada (also known as Lefkas,

1400 BCE
The Mycenaeans, who are considered to be early Greeks, settle on the islands.

395–1204
Eastern Roman Empire to Byzantine era. The islands belong to Byzantium.

1386
The Venetians take control of Corfu, followed by Zakynthos in 1482, Kefalonia in 1500 and Ithaca in 1503. Lefkada falls to the Ottomans in 1467 and later, in 1684, to Venice.

1815–64
The Ionian Islands become a republic under a British protectorate.

1864
Union with Greece.

north of Kefalonia, is only a few kilometres from the Greek mainland. Then, finally, there is Kithira, southeast of the Peloponnese Peninsula, far from the main islands. And there are also countless tiny islands.

NATURAL WONDERS

Unlike many of the Aegean Islands, the Ionian Islands are fertile and relatively green. Large areas are covered with ancient olive groves and dark, slender cypress trees that punctuate the forest of silver leaves that shimmer in the sun, lending the hilly landscape an air of relaxed serenity. In some places there are dense pine forests – such as on Mount Ainos on Kefalonia, which has been declared a national park. The diversity of the landscape attracts those who enjoy hiking and other outdoor activities. Winding mountain roads offer breathtaking views of the sea, with the silhouettes of neighbouring islands visible on the horizon. On Kefalonia, you can also explore beautiful limestone caves, and there is always a fresh breeze around the light-flooded sea caves of Zakynthos.

WATER SPORTS FOR ALL

You can plunge into the pleasantly cool sea from bays and coves with long ribbons of fine sand and pebbles. This natural environment, with its interplay of colours between land and sea, is unparalleled in Europe. If you love the ocean, you can sail, surf, dive and do all kinds of other water sports. Some beaches are not just popular with holidaymakers but also with turtles. In the marine national park on southern Zakynthos, environmentalists have set strict rules to ensure that the turtle

1941-44
Occupation by Italian and German troops.

1953
Devastating earthquake.

1967-74
Military dictatorship.

2010-2019
Greece is particularly hard hit by the global economic crisis.

2014
An earthquake damages more than a thousand buildings on Kefalonia.

2020
Tornado on Kefalonia.

2020/2021
Tourism experiences a Covid-induced break.

offspring have a safe haven. Meanwhile, sun worshippers find their paradise in Laganas on Zakynthos, on the Paliki Peninsula on Kefalonia, on Kathisma Beach on Lefkada or – after a short boat ride – next to the legendary shipwreck at Navagio.

WINE, OLIVES, TOURISTS AND LOTS OF SHEEP

Corfu (see the Marco Polo *Corfu* guide) is the most populous and economically strongest of the Ionian Islands (pop. 103,000), but it is not the only one that is well developed for tourism. During the summer there are more tourists than locals on Lefkada and Zakynthos. However, on Kefalonia and Ithaca, tourism plays second fiddle. On both islands, agriculture has the more important role, with more goats and sheep than tourists; on Kefalonia, Lefkada and Zakynthos olives and grapes (for wine) are grown. Although there are fishermen everywhere, they cannot even meet the needs of the locals with their catch.

NO GREEK CLICHÉS HERE

There are few archaeological excavations of national importance on the islands – due to their remote location they were not an important area during antiquity. In the Middle Ages they formed part of Byzantium, and thereafter Venice. The Ionian Islands have the Venetians to thank for the fact that – with the exception of Lefkada which is closer to the Greek mainland – they were never under Ottoman rule, unlike the rest of Greece. As a result, there are no Ottoman remnants, such as mosques or bathhouses, on the islands. Instead Venetian-influenced arcades and multi-storey houses are typical elements of Ionian architecture, reflecting the style of the commerce-driven city state. Artists came to the Ionian Islands, inspired by Italian style: thus the Ionian School of art was born. Dating from the mid-17th century, it combined Byzantine and Western traditions. The best overview of the school can be seen in the Zakynthos Museum.

In addition to Venice, Britain also played a role in the fact that the Ionian Islands are different from the rest of the Greece. Napoleon conquered Venice in 1797, and during that same year he placed the islands under French rule. Over the next few years, the islands had a succession of rulers – France, Russia and England – until the Congress of Vienna in 1815, when they were declared a British protectorate as the Republic of Seven Islands. The 49 years as a British colony meant that the archipelago was provided with a good road network and modern water supply to the towns. However, the islanders repeatedly revolted against foreign rule and supported the rest of Greece in its battle for freedom from the Ottomans, which was won in 1832. They pushed for the unification of their islands with free Greece, and in 1864 Corfu and the other Ionian Islands were finally united with mainland Greece.

The serenity and ease of island life has remained a characteristic feature to this day. This includes cool music festivals just as much as meditation on the beach, services in the local monastery, or dining in an elegant restaurant as the sun disappears behind the horizon.

AT A GLANCE

208,000
inhabitants (including Corfu)

Crete: approx. 650,000

624km
of coastline

UK mainland: 17,800km

1,200 NESTS
are dug by the loggerhead turtles each year in the bay of Laganas

AROUND 80
days of rainfall annually on Zakynthos

(LONDON: 170 DAYS)

7.5 HOURS
OF SUNSHINE EACH DAY

(LONDON: 4 HOURS)

LOCAL VARIETY OF GRAPE:
ROBOLA
GROWING REGION: KEFALONIA

THERE ARE 7 MAIN IONIAN ISLANDS
Capital: Corfu
Largest island: Kefalonia

MOUNT AINOS (KEFALONIA)
Highest mountain
1,628m

FAMOUS PEOPLE
ODYSSEUS (mythological hero)
IOANNIS METAXAS (prime minister, dictator)
DIONYSIOS SOLOMOS (poet, author of the text of the Greek national anthem)

UNDERSTAND THE IONIAN ISLANDS

ICONS

In the Orthodox Church icons are the representations of Jesus, the Virgin Mary, saints and biblical events on panel paintings. They are found in all Orthodox churches, but also in private homes and in vehicles, offices, classrooms and doctors' surgeries. Icons are viewed differently from the religious images in Western churches. They are seen as a "window to heaven", and are said to bring the saints into the home, making them ever-present. They are venerated, kissed and decorated with precious metals, embroidered curtains, precious stones, rings and watches. In short, icons are treated as if they were the saints themselves.

AGIA, AGIOS

Travellers will see the words *Agia*, *Agii* and *Agios* everywhere. They are part of the names of villages and churches, fishing boats and car ferries. *Agios* means saint, *Agia* is the female form and *Agii* the plural of both. The Virgin Mary has a special honorary name, *Panagia*, the Most Holy.

FOLK BELIEFS & SUPERSTITION

In Greece, as in many countries, there is a widespread fear of the evil eye: a curse is believed to be transferable to another person through a person's gaze. The cursed person then suffers from nausea, lack of energy or migraine. However, the curse can be broken by a gifted individual (who is usually from the victim's own family or village) who conducts a special ceremony using oil and water. Many local people wear a blue *mati* (Greek: eye) for protection. You will also find this symbol as a charm in all kinds of rooms or vehicles.

Elderly men, in particular, like to play with a *komboloi*, a chain of beads similar to a rosary. It has no religious significance, but is meant to bring its bearer luck and also serves as a way to pass the time. The Greeks probably modified theirs from Turkish prayer beads; Greek worry beads always have an uneven number, usually 13 or 17.

BYZANTIUM – ISLANDS AS A PART OF THE EMPIRE

The term "Byzantium" is rarely used these days. It is the name given to an empire that existed for more than 1,000 years and kept many of the values and achievements of the ancient world alive well into the late Middle Ages. Byzantium was originally a city (today's Istanbul) founded by Greeks around 660 BCE. It became the capital of the Eastern Roman Empire after its separation from Rome, capital of the Western Roman Empire. Its symbol was a two-headed bird. The Greek Orthodox Church, one of the country's main institutions, still carries an image of the imperial Byzantine double-headed eagle on its flags, maintaining a spiritual connection

Icon wall paintings in the Zakynthos Museum in Zakynthos Town

with Byzantium. You can see flags with this symbol outside churches, monasteries, monuments and forts. The Ionian Islands were a part of the Byzantine Empire until the early 12th century. It was an empire that, at its peak, stretched as far as Italy, North Africa and Asia Minor. It played an essential role in the Greek national story because, over time, Christianity came to be the state religion. Being part of the empire also helped a modern Greek language to develop, creating a common language, which was essential for the emergence of a national identity. On the islands, the influence of Byzantium is present in many churches and countless chapels with distinctive Byzantine, Orthodox appearance. Many typically Greek church buildings feature the Byzantine style of a cross-shaped outline with a round dome. When new frescoes and icons are created today, the Byzantine style is often imitated. And Byzantine-style jewellery is also popular.

TRACES OF VENETIAN RULE

If Zakynthos or Argostoli remind you of dreamy Italian harbour towns, this is easily explained: for almost 600 years the islands belonged to the Venetian maritime republic. The Venetians called the islands the Levantines, or "Eastern Isles". Being part of Venice meant that there was little in the way of influence from the Ottomans; instead, Western cultural influence dominated. The building style, which is characteristic of the Italian Renaissance, and the brightly

Sustainable electricity generation on Kefalonia

pastel-coloured façades, are living expression of this era. You can also discover hall-like churches that are built in the Italian style. Some have tall, freestanding bell towers, which are uncommon in the rest of Greece. Italian or Venetian was even the official language at one time, and when mixed with Greek, a local dialect developed. Today, you can detect some of these phrases in the *kantades*, the folk tunes that are accompanied by a guitar and best enjoyed in a taverna with a glass of Italian-style wine, like a Verdea or Robola. The Robola grape variety isn't grown any longer in Italy itself, but only survives in the Ionian Islands.

BEACH LIFE

In summer, a dip in the sea is an almost-daily occurrence for most islanders, and the quality of beaches and their water is a popular local topic of conversation. Most islanders go to a taverna after their swim – or to one of the modern beach bars for a drink and snack served in lounge chairs.

Lifeguards are only available on a few of the more popular beaches, and then only during high season. The majority of maintained beaches on Zakynthos are in the south, and the island has a total of 14 Blue Flags, with 13 on Kefalonia and eight on Lefkada. Beaches are rated every year in terms of water quality, safety and environmental management.

Although sun loungers and umbrellas are rented out on many of the beaches, you can also just lie on your towel if you prefer. The deck-chair renters and taverna owners usually clean their beaches, and when money is available, so do the local municipalities. Private beaches have been allowed since 2014, but they are still few in number.

EARTHQUAKES

Mild earthquakes are common on the Ionian Islands. However, a catastrophic earthquake hit the southern islands in 1953, destroying 94 per cent of homes on Zakynthos, 91 per cent on Kefalonia, and 70 per cent on Ithaca. This is the reason why so few villages on these islands have any traditional architecture. Foreign aid and wealthy shipping magnates facilitated earthquake-proof reconstruction.

RENEWABLE ENERGY

Greece has wind and sun in abundance, yet both are not used nearly enough for energy production. Solar panels are widely used to heat water in private households and hotels, but photovoltaic systems for energy production, which were pioneered by Greece on Crete, are still nearly absent on the Ionian Islands. However, investment in renewable energy is high on the political agenda, and Greece intends to increase renewables' share in total energy generation to 35 per cent by 2030. Instead of solar power from photovoltaic plants, the Greeks favour the generation of electricity from wind power. On

TRUE OR FALSE?

ALWAYS THE SAME NAMES

Are all Greeks called Kostas? Obviously not, but while the younger generation has lost its appetite for carrying on the same old names, the tradition that children are named after their grandparents is still followed to some extent. Every year, children's name-giving saints are honoured with a big celebration, often including cousins who have the same name. What may sound like trendy names tend not to give anything away about your social background but are more likely to indicate your origin: St Dionysis is the patron saint of Zakynthos, and many men on Kefalonia are named after St Gerasimos.

TIMING ISSUES

In Greece, punctuality is a matter of personal judgement. When it comes to a date, boat trip, hike or visit to the taverna, people always seem to have an answer with regard to the time like "in ten minutes", but these ten minutes may extend or contract depending on the situation. Even at a concert or the theatre, performances don't necessarily start "on time". Sadly, though, you can't rely on the fact that someone will be on time either… However, slowing down is good for the soul, especially on holiday.

Kefalonia, three wind parks already feed electricity into the power grid, and on the other islands, wind turbines – largely funded by the EU – also add to the reduction in petroleum products used in the mostly outdated island power plants. The islands of Corfu, Kefalonia, Lefkada and Zakynthos are still connected to the mainland via an underwater power cable, but this is soon to change. The signs are pointing in the direction of the islands using electricity generated from solar, wind and hydroelectric power.

CRISIS

Between 2010 and 2019, Greece was plunged into a debt crisis, which affected almost all sections of society. Many taxes were raised and wages, pensions and social benefits were cut. This caused a great deal of hardship, and many Greeks moved to wealthier European countries to escape unemployment.

Throughout the crisis and beyond, lotteries have remained popular and tickets are available everywhere, including scratch cards with instant wins. The state lottery jackpot is up for grabs every Wednesday and Saturday. Lottery ticket sellers are just as much a common sight on the islands as Orthodox priests or street stalls. In fact, it's a common way for pensioners to top up their now-meagre incomes.

No negative economic news can spoil dream-like beaches, and even as the Greek economy was in crisis, the tourist industry continued to boom to the extent that, on Zakynthos, people started to complain about excessive visitor numbers. And when refugees from war-torn countries crossed the Aegean Sea in 2015 to apply for asylum in Europe, causing tourist numbers to drop on other islands that had turned into refugee hotspots, the Ionian Islands continued to break visitor records.

The Covid-19 crisis of 2020–21 changed the situation once again, with holiday seasons cut short and lower visitor numbers. However, even tornado Ianos, which hit the islands in September 2020 causing considerable damage, didn't put the tourists off altogether, and numbers have since picked up.

A monument to the hero of Homer's *The Odyssey* in Vathi on Ithaca

ODYSSEUS

In contrast to the other characters in Homer's *Iliad*, all of whom impress with their physical strength in war, Odysseus was a thinker – he was the one who came up with the idea of the Trojan Horse. Originally, the Trojan Horse was not well-camouflaged malware on a personal computer, but a huge, hollow wooden horse on wheels left outside the walls of Troy. Believing it to be an offering, the Trojans wheeled it into their city, whereupon the soldiers hiding inside jumped out and vanquished the Trojans. It was only then that Homer's hero was able to return home, but not on any direct route: his odyssey lasted a full ten years, during which he and his crew sailed the entire Mediterranean Sea. He lost all of his companions, but also got to know some goddesses along the way.

In the end, Odysseus was shipwrecked on Corfu, where the local ruler of the Phaeacians gave him a boat which brought him back to his home – the island he ruled for many years. But which island is that? Where did he return to? This question has been the subject of an academic dispute forever. Ithaca is mentioned in the epic, and has long considered itself Odysseus's home, but Kefalonia also carried the same name once upon a time. Archaeological finds, coins and graves prove that both islands have traces of the hero's presence. Fans of this epic – which has been translated into many languages as well as interpreted in art and movies – can admire the traces of Odysseus on both islands, which are direct neighbours.

EATING
SHOPPING
SPORT

Romantic dining beside the sea in Assos, on Kefalonia

EATING & DRINKING

Greek cuisine is down to earth and tasty. Pasta dishes add an Italian touch to Ionian cooking, which is further broadened with creations from Anatolia. All the islands have a wide selection of restaurants. Many are open from noon to midnight, while others serve lunch until 6pm or are only open in the evening. Barbecue stalls and bakeries offer snacks throughout the day.

FOR MEAT LOVERS
However varied a menu is, meat dishes often form the main course. Apart from *souvlaki* (skewers) and other grilled meats, meatballs and fried liver *(sikoti)*, you may enjoy juicy baked or pot dishes such as *juvarlakia* (meat dumplings with rice) or *juvetsi* (rice-shaped noodles with beef). A regional favourite is *kreatópita*: a meat pie with tomatoes, rice and cheese, encased in pastry.

Try the local lamb, mutton or goat – there is no more natural location for the sure-footed animals than on these mountainous islands! The same goes for fish and seafood which, while not exactly cheap, are as fresh as it gets. The menu often lists a price per kilogramme for fish – it's a good idea to check beforehand how much your portion will cost.

FOR VEGETARIANS
Vegetarians will feel at home with Greek cuisine. *Magirefta* – one-pot casseroles cooked with plenty of olive oil – include vegan dishes made with giant beans *(gigantes)*, chickpeas *(rewihia)* and green beans *(fasolia)*. Restaurants of the same name, which are open during the day in the towns, serve generous vegetarian portions at reasonable prices. Actually, visiting the islands just before Easter is the ideal time for a vegetarian diet

A hearty main course: *stifado* (beef stew) and a sweet spicy dessert: *ladópita*

because during Lent local people turn vegan (*nistisimo*) and typical meat dishes are converted into delicious vegetarian options.

EAT LIKE THE LOCALS

Good tavernas – traditional restaurants – also attract local people. If the establishment serves predominantly fish, it is called *psarotaverna*. Because of the warm climate, Greeks tend to eat dinner from 9pm onwards and then sit together until late at night. The communal meal is a focal point of life, and people deeply appreciate the *parea* (getting together). Wine is drunk from small water glasses and the toast is "Stin ijia mas" – to our health! Frequently, dishes are placed in the centre of the table and people help themselves, and the bill is paid jointly. However, if somebody insists on splitting the bill into individual accounts, that is acceptable too. Any

leftovers may be taken home as a *paketo* for another day.

FOOD ON THE GO

You can't go wrong with a *pita* (flat-bread) at the *gyradiko* or at stalls that serve falafel, *bougatsa* and *tiropita* (sweet and savoury filled pastries), or sandwich shops and crêperies. Most of them have somewhere to sit down so that you don't have to eat your snack while standing.

SNACK CULTURE – KAFENIO & CO

Traditional restaurants such as *kafenia*, *ouzerie* and *mezodopolia*, all of which are pretty much the same kind of establishment, offer snacks. Here you can sit comfortably, often enjoy live *bouzouki* music in the evening and feast on freshly prepared snacks (*mezedes*).

The old-style coffee house (*kafenio*), full of men, has largely become a choice, although nobody would say no to alcohol here either. The selection is added to by Greek and Dutch draught beer. Regional brands from microbreweries are available in modern *kafenias*, whereas for a glass of top-quality wine you will need to visit a restaurant or winery.

INSIDER TIP
Beer lover's heaven

SWEET DELIGHTS – COFFEE & CAKE

After your dinner in a taverna, the owner will often serve something sweet on the house. Cakes are sweetened with plenty of syrup. Home-made regional sweets such as *mantolato* (white nougat) and *pasteli* (sesame bar) are available in bakeries.

If you order a cup of coffee, you need to specify how sweet you want it: *elliniko* (Greek coffee) is boiled together with the sugar. It comes in many variations: *sketo* (without sugar), *metrio* (with a little sugar), *gliko* (with lots of sugar), *diplo* (as double) or *me gala* (with milk). In the streets, you will often see people carrying a coffee cup which contains cold frappe – frothed instant coffee. However, Italy comes out on top in the coffee stakes: *freddo espresso* is the drink of choice, served in large glasses with lots of ice. This should give you plenty of energy to last for the day!

Olives and ouzo are a must for perfect holiday vibes!

thing of the past. In the towns, a new kind of establishment has emerged, with a more adventurous menu: salty grilled cheese with jam, grilled sausage with a hint of orange, or octopus with chilli. To make the delicious food go down more easily, people drink a house wine, wine with resin *(retsina)* or spirits *(tsipouro, ouzo)* from carafes. In the *kafenio*, coffee is the drink of

Today's specials

Starters

FAVA WITH CAPERS
Purée made with yellow split peas

GRAVIERA WITH TOMATO JAM
Hard cheese made of goat's or sheep's milk, similar to Swiss Gruyère

GARIDES SAGANAKI
Pan-fried shrimps in tomato and ouzo sauce

Snacks & street food

PATSARIA
Fresh beetroot, boiled and served in vinegar and oil

SOUVLAKI
Grilled pork or chicken skewers

Main courses

KREATOPITA
A Kefalonian delicacy: meat pie with lamb or pork baked with rice, herbs, onions, tomatoes and cheese, encased in pastry

BOURDETO
Peppery, red fish soup

BRIAM
Soft baked vegetables (courgettes, aubergines, tomatoes, potatoes, red peppers, red onions) with garlic

Desserts

LADOPITA
Lefkadian oil cake with honey, cinnamon, cloves and sesame

MANTOLATO
White nougat without any cocoa but with almond brittle, from Zakynthos

Drinks

OUZO/TSIPOURO
Spirit made with solid remains of wine-making grapes, clear or with an aniseed-and-fennel spice blend (*me glikaniso*)

SPITIKI LIMONADA
Home-made lemonade

ROBOLA
Dry white wine from Kefalonia, with a lemon scent

SHOPPING

On the islands, shopping for agricultural produce by the wayside is commonplace. In summer, shops are open daily until 11pm. During the off-season, retailers have a lunch break between 2pm and 5.30pm. Apart from mass-produced items, the souvenir shops and small stores sell real arts and crafts. By the way, bargaining is always an option.

PEASANT GOLD: OLIVE OIL

The best Greek olive oil is available in all the island towns. Don't forget you'll need to pack it in your hold luggage due to airline regulations for the transport of liquids in hand luggage (100ml per container). Otherwise, you can buy larger quantities at the airport after passing through security. If you have run out of space, some manufacturers such as Daphnes (*daphnes-zakynthos.com/products.html*) on Zakynthos will send oil to your home address.

ALMONDS

The Paliki Peninsula on Kefalonia is famous for its 🚩 almond specialities: *mandoles* (roasted) and *barboulé* (caramelised) almonds. No visitor leaves Zakynthos without *pastelli*, sweet sesame and honey bars, or *mandolato*, a soft variety of nougat. The small currants found on Zakynthos and Kefalonia are also delicious.

WINE & SPIRITS

There is a good selection of Greek wines in the *cava* shops in the towns. On Zakynthos, Kefalonia and Lefkada you can visit wineries and buy wine directly 🐖 at cost. Lefkada and Argostoli have shops that sell own-made liqueurs, brandy and ouzo, sometimes straight from the barrel.

Zakynthos to take away: cloths with a marine motif and olive-wood cutlery

STRAIGHT FROM THE TRADER

The older generation sell their goods by the roadside: fruit, vegetables, teas, herbs, jams, syrup, honey, noodles and liqueurs – all home-made. You may find very reasonably priced 🐖 🐄 regional agricultural souvenirs. And if you are self-catering, the weekly market is just perfect *(Lefkada Sat, Zakynthos Mon, Thu, Sat)*.

GLITTERING JEWELLERY, CHARMS & MORE

You can find handmade leather and shell jewellery on the coastal promenades, while jewellery stores offer elegant Byzantine-style gold pieces and items made with semi-precious stones. Whatever price bracket you are looking at, jewellery is cheaper than at home and can be found in all the towns.

Serenity can also be bought on the islands: the *mati* (blue-eye charm) is said to protect you from the "evil eye", and is available in many guises, from pendants to bracelets and even cushions. Letting the *komboloi* chain run through your hands is supposed to help with a nervous disposition (see p. 20, Understand).

INSIDER TIP
Mosaics to go

A real eye-catcher are trendy handbags adorned with colourful mosaic stones. You can find these in, for example, Fiskardo and Argostoli on Kefalonia.

And if you are in need of divine intervention, there are wooden pocket icons for sale in religious shops at churches and monasteries.

SPORT & ACTIVITIES

Brave the waves, climb mountains, hike along steep cliffs. Endless coastlines, high hills and deep valleys provide ideal conditions for outdoor sports, whether you're experienced or a newcomer. The islands are a paradise for sailors, surfers and divers, while mountain bikers and hikers will find wonderful scenic routes.

BIKING

Kefalonia and Lefkada are ideal for ambitious mountain bikers; there are still several tracks in the mountains that have, at the most, only been explored by a few jeeps. But don't underestimate the ascents!

On Kefalonia you can get a bike and good tips at *Aionos Bicycle Store (Odos Sitemporon 61–63 | Argostoli | tel. 26 71 02 68 74 | ainosbicycles.gr)*. They also rent out good child seats and even bicycle trailers. Guided tours are operated by *Fiora Bikes (fiorabikes. gr)*.

On Lefkada, *Get active (getactive lefkas.com)* offers daily mountain bike guided tours of different lengths and difficulty levels. Road bikes are also available for hire. All resorts on Zakynthos also have places to hire bikes, mountain bikes and e-bikes *(go-electric.eu)*. The latter are ideal on mountainous Ithaca *(Ithaki Alpha Bike and Car Rental | Vathi | tel. 26 74 03 28 50)*.

DIVING & SNORKELLING

Pleasant water temperatures make scuba diving around the islands a possibility all year round. Snorkelling is feasible in all good diving spots, such as along the coastline pitted with caves on the peninsula in the south-west of Limni Keriou on Zakynthos. There are two 🦩 dive centres with a lot of experience: *Turtle Beach Diving*

The island of Lefkada is a kitesurfer's paradise

Centre, Timotheos Marmiris (Limni Keriou | harbour | tel. 26 95 04 87 68 | diving-center-turtle-beach.com) and the Nero Sport Diving Center (Limni Keriou, west of the harbour | tel. 26 95 02 84 81 | nero-sport.de).

In the west of Kefalonia dives can turn into sightseeing at an Italian shipwreck from World War II, final resting place to 2,000 soldiers (Lixouri Peninsula | pirate-divers-club.gr).

Diving schools on Lefkada include Lefkas Diving Center (Nikiana | tel. 26 45 07 21 05 | lefkasdivingcenter. gr) and Nautilus (Vassiliki | tel. 69 36 18 17 75 | underwater.gr). Ithaca also has operators, such as Odyssey Outdoor Activities (Vathi | tel. 69 48 18 26 55 | outdoorithaca.com).

FISHING

Fishing is fun with the right instruction. Professional fisherman Dimitrios, who lives in Katelios on Kefalonia,

takes guests on fishing cruises (Kato Katelios | tel. 69 47 66 75 95 | fishing tourismkefalonia.com). Otherwise let Michalis (Agia Pelagia | tel. 69 55 58 85 56 | michalisfishingtourism. com) take you. The tour departs from Katelios around 8am and returns at 2pm. The freshly caught fish will be served for lunch. There are also tours with subsequent lunch on Zakynthos (gofishing.gr, zantefishingtours.gr). They start at 7am, or there are sunset tours for those who like to lie in.

HIKING

Hiking in the Ionian mountains is wonderful. There are no accurate hiking maps, and only a few marked trails on Kefalonia (especially near Fiskardo and around Mount Ainos). Therefore, it may be a good idea to employ a skilled guide (outdoorkefalonia.com). If you are familiar with the area, you can increase your speed to

Fiskardo on Kefalonia is not just a harbour for big boats

sporting levels. There are also knowledgeable guides on Ithaca *(tours from 40 euros | outdoorithaca.com)*.

PARAGLIDING & COASTEERING

When paragliding on Lefkada, you take off towards the sea from a mountain *(tandem, approx. 80 euros)*. There are several operators to choose from. The starting point at the Rachi restaurant is at a height of 600m *(Exanthia | Kathisma Beach | flylefkada. gr, lefkadaparagliding.gr, rachi.gr)*. It's a great experience!

You need to be in good physical shape for coasteering on Kefalonia *(approx. 45 euros)*. Jump into refreshing waters and climb up and down rocks in a wetsuit and helmet *(Argostoli | outdoorkefalonia.com)*.

RIDING

Experience the thrill of galloping across a beach and into the water. For riding enthusiasts there are some excellent stables at Zervata on Kefalonia. Owner Cornelia Schimpfky stables sure-footed Haflinger horses and offers rides – from several hours to multi-day – as well as lessons in jumping and dressage *(tel. 69 77 53 32 03 | kephalonia.com)*. In Sami (Kefalonia) you can go on rides and trails over several days *(kefalonias horseridingstable.com)*.

On Zakynthos, the horse-crazy Tsourakis family *(off the Argassi– Kalamaki road | tel. 69 77 87 57 92 | laganahorseriding.gr)* has more than 50 ponies and horses for beginners and experienced riders alike. On guided tours you ride through the Laganas valley, pine forests and sand dunes to the sea. For 👹 those who weigh less than 55kg, a donkey ride on Kefalonia is a lot of fun. The rides on the sensitive animals are designed to be "hikes in company" (see p. 75).

WATER SPORTS

There are water sport centres on all of the islands where you can rent pedal boats, or go waterskiing and kitesurfing. Stand-up paddleboarding is also popular. Guided SUP tours are available from Nidri (Lefkada) to the island of *Meganisi (tel. 69 81 49 79 21 | lefkadapaddleboardcruises.com)*.

At *Milos Windsurf Club (Agios Ioannis, Lefkada | tel. 26 45 02 13 32 | milosbeach.gr)* you can be taken out on a jet ski or try an exciting hydrofoil.

Motor boat rentals are big business on all four islands and anyone above 18 years old can hire 30hp motor boats without a boat licence or previous experience. After a short briefing, you can set sail for beaches and islands that would be otherwise inaccessible. The cost of daily hire depends on the horse power you choose and the season, varying between 70 and 140 euros/day. You can find operators in nearly every resort and at every port.

SAILING

Sail in yachting heaven! You can hire a sailing boat in the marinas *(booking recommended, see below)*. Also, flotilla sailing is available from Palairos (mainland opposite Lefkada) with operators *Sailpoint (sailpoint.org)* and *Sunsail (sunsail.de)*. The cruises take one or two weeks and even offer the beginner the opportunity to sail the area alone, as the experienced crew ensure safety from an accompanying boat.

INSIDER TIP
Chartering for beginners

As a passenger you can watch the skipper and maybe learn a few tricks! Starting points are the marina on Lefkada with *Oasis Sailing (tel. 69 45 59 86 36 | oasisailing.com)* or Nidri (Lefkada) with *Skorpios Charter (tel. 26 45 09 22 81 | skorpioscharter.com)*.

WINDSURFING

On Lefkada many beaches have windsurfing centres. One of the good ones is

INSIDER TIP
Against the wind

Club Vassiliki (Vassiliki beach | tel. 26 45 03 15 88 | clubvass.com), where children can go on courses and beginners train on dry land to start with. The very windy area around *Milos Windsurf Club (Agios Ioannis near Lefkada Town | tel. 26 45 02 13 32 | milosbeach.gr)* is better suited to experienced surfers, although some beginners will appreciate the challenge.

REGIONAL OVERVIEW

LEFKADA p. 86

Greek life at its best: parties, beaches and sport

Combine excitement with relaxation on Odysseus's fabled isle

KEFALONIA p. 62

So very green: sweet dreams amid lush flora and fauna

ITHACA P.

ZAKYNTHOS p. 40

Unforgettable encounters with nature and an elegant lifestyle

Thyamis

Louros

Amvrakikos Kolpos

Limn Amvraki

Preveza

Lefkada

Lefkada (Lefkas)

Vassiliki

I O N I O

P E L A G O S

Fiskardo

Frikes

Ithaki

Vathi

Argostoli

Kefalonia

Skala

Killini

Korithi

ZAKYNTHOS

Zakynthos

Keri

20 km
12.43 mi

ZAKYNTHOS

WINE, BEACHES, TURTLES

The Venetians called their southernmost territory in the Ionian Sea *Fior di Levante*, "Flower of the East". The 406-km² island is noted for its fertility, its good wines and for being an outdoor lover's paradise.

However, today's visitors to Zakynthos come especially for the amazing sandy beaches. The most beautiful, those on the Bay of Laganas, have also been sought out since time immemorial by sea turtles, who visit to lay their eggs. Protected areas have been

Shipwreck Beach is the top postcard image in Greece

established to give these beautiful animals a refuge. Venture out to sea to meet the turtles, peek into the sparkling blue caves or reach the extremely scenic Shipwreck Beach. If these stunning destinations aren't enough, what about a visit to one of the many wineries on the island, including a tasting session? Beach bars provide a great atmosphere, and there are all kinds of water sports available for all levels. And if you want to experience solitude, you can climb to retreats in the hills at heights of up to 756m.

ZAKYNTHOS

7 Blue Caves (Galazia Spilea) ★

Ormos Skinari

6 Agios Nikolaos/ Cape Skinari

Βαρβάρα
Varvara

25 mins–2 hrs

Άνω Βολίμες
Ano Volimes

Volimes **8**

Makris Gialos

10

9

**Shipwreck Beach
(Navagio)** ★

Agios Georgiou
Krimnon Monastery

Ορθονιές
Orthonies

*Ormos
Alikon*

Αλυκανά
Alykana

11 Anafonitria Monastery

Ε Λ Λ Α Σ
G R E E C E

Alykes **4**

12 Porto Vromi

Μαρίες
Maries

Pigadakia **5**

*Ormos
Stenitis*

Γύρι
Gyri

13 Exo Choria

*Ormos
Shiza*

Loucha **18**

30km, 45 mins

14 Kambi

Αγία Μαρίν
Agia Marin

Άγιος Λέων
Agios Leon

Κοιλιωμένο
Killomeno

*Ormos
Katevasma*

15 Porto Limnionas

16 Porto Roxa

*Ormos
Limniona*

Ι Ο Ν Ι Ο
Π Ε Λ Α Γ Ο Σ

Agalas **17**

Ι Ο Ν Ι Ο
PELAGOS

3 km
1.86 mi

MARCO POLO HIGHLIGHTS

★ **ZAKYNTHOS MUSEUM**
Ionian style: typical historic paintings from the islands ➤ p. 45

★ **BOCHALI**
Pine trees within ruined medieval walls and fantastic views of the capital from the cliff ➤ p. 45

★ **BLUE CAVES (GALAZIA SPILEA)**
A magical swim in a beautiful setting ➤ p. 47

★ **SHIPWRECK BEACH (NAVAGIO)**
A beautiful and isolated cove, with a shipwreck on the beach, which can only be reached by boat ➤ p. 47

★ **VARKAROLA**
Genuine Zakynthian *kantades* sung every evening ➤ p. 61

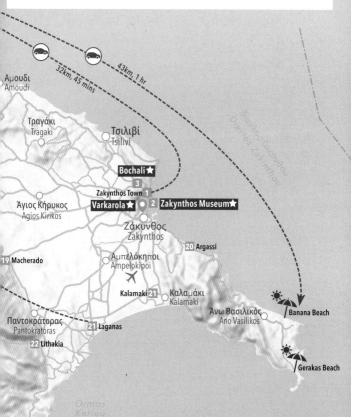

In the evening, head to Zakynthos Town, where Italianate *kantades* or folk songs are sung in lively tavernas. They play international hits too: time doesn't stand still on this island!

1 ZAKYNTHOS TOWN

After the earthquake of 1953, Zakynthos Town (pop. 11,000) had to be completely rebuilt. Fortunately, the result is not an ugly 1950s-style town, but a good mix of historical reconstruction and appealing new buildings. The only sightseeing options, though, are the museums, as well as a few interesting churches. But a stroll through the Mediterranean town is just lovely and the view from the harbour promenade is serene.

On the other side of the road from the promenade, the row of buildings is home to simple tavernas, cafés, tourist kiosks with stacks of cuddly toys, and travel agents offering information on boat trips around the island.

At the western end of the coastal road is the largest and most important *church* in town, dedicated to the island saint Dionisyios. This church was repainted in the traditional Byzantine style in the 1980s. Parts of the frescoes depict scenes from the life and work of the saint, who was born on Zakynthos in 1547 and died here in 1622. The western façade is adorned with modern mosaics depicting the patron saints of three Ionian Islands: Saint Spyridon of Corfu, Saint Gerasimos of Kefalonia and Saint Dionysios of Zakynthos. The remains of the island's saint are particularly revered and lie in a magnicent silver sarcophagus. It stands in a side chapel to the right of the chancel *(daily 7.30am–1pm, 5–7.30pm)*. In the adjoining building is the island's *Bishop's Palace*.

The rows of houses are pretty, with ordered pedestrian alleyways and various shops. Continue to the *Platia Agiou Markou* with its many cafés and the small *San Marcus* church, where a Roman Catholic mass takes place every Sunday at 7pm in the summer. The painting above the altar is said to be by Titian or one of his students.

If you walk a few steps east from the Platia Agou Markou, you will come across the *Mitropolis*, the town's cathedral. It is decorated with magnificent frescoes in the traditional Byzantine style. Continue from the Mitropolis towards the sea, turn left at the first intersection and you will see the very beautiful portal of the *Kiria ton Angelon* church dating back to 1687. Right on the coast is the large *Platia Solomou* and the church of the patron saint of seafarers, the *Agios Nikolaos*. It was built in 1560 with funding by the local fishermen's guild.

When you return to the town centre, take *Odos Tertseti* street and on your left-hand side you will find a small piece of land where the island's synagogue once stood. It was founded in 1489 by the Jewish community but was destroyed in 1953 by the earthquake. Two memorials *(Odos Tertseti 44)* commemorate the island's Orthodox bishop and the mayor of Zakynthos at the time of the German

Fishing boats moored in the port of Zakynthos Town

occupation during World War II. They bravely resisted the Nazi order to supply a list of their Jewish fellow citizens, and in so doing saved them from evacuation to the German extermination camps.

Afterwards have a break high up at the *Kastro* (castle) and enjoy the impressive scenic views. *F16–17*

2 ZAKYNTHOS MUSEUM ★ ⚑

The eye-catching museum on Solomos Square provides a detailed overview of the history of painting on the Ionian Islands and especially of the works of the so-called Ionian School of the 17th to 19th centuries, which was strongly influenced by Italian painting. A relief model and historical photos show what the town looked like before the

earthquake in 1953. *Tue–Sat 8am–3pm | admission 4 euros | Zakynthos Town | Platia Solomou | ⏱ 1½ hrs | F16–17*

3 BOCHALI ★

The village on the long range of hills above the island capital is the ideal destination for late afternoon and early evening. First, you can visit the sprawling Venetian *Fortress Bochali* (*May–Oct Mon, Wed–Sat 8.30am–4pm | admission 4 euros*), which is almost completely overgrown with pine trees, forming a real forest. The outer walls and the gates are well preserved, but little remains of the other buildings, such as the storerooms, churches and barracks.

After visiting the fortress, you can

Collector's joy at the Folk Museum Pigadakia

take a stroll (400m) to the main village square. The view over the town, the harbour and the Peloponnese is terrific. *E16*

4 ALYKES

This coastal village is particularly popular with British holidaymakers. It is only sparsely developed and lies on the edge of a disused salt flat right on a miles-long narrow sandy beach that is great for jogging and cycling. In the evening there are almost more horse-drawn carriages than cars on the road and the prices here are remarkably low. The small fishing port at the mouth of the river is especially charming. Old stone houses harbour tavernas and restaurants serving international cuisine. Approximately 150m

upstream a six-arched Venetian-era bridge spans the river. *E16*

5 PIGADAKIA

Former cattle farmer Spiros Vertzagio has been collecting historic items on the island for almost 30 years, from household goods to agricultural equipment, and displays everything in his *Folk Museum (daily 9am–9pm | admission 3 euros | Pigadakia, road to Alykes | ⏱ 30 mins)*, a reconstruction of a traditional Zykanthian house. In his own cheerful way, Vertzagio comments

INSIDER TIP
A bit of a flea market

on religious, political and even somewhat pornographic items, images and newspapers. Spiros also runs a traditional taverna in the village centre, where he sells local produce such as currants, olive oil and wine.

The sound of splashing water is everywhere in the village as it has numerous springs, including a sulphurous spring under the altar of the small *chapel* opposite the taverna. Believers and the sick draw water from it. You can enjoy the home-made red wine and *souvlaki* on a tour by miniature train that is also owned by Spiros *(12 euros | trainaki.com | tour takes approx. 2 hrs). ⚏ E16*

6 AGIOS NIKOLAOS/ CAPE SKINARI

The little village on the Bay of Skinari only has 40 permanent residents, but is the second most important harbour on the island. This is where the excursion boats leave for the Blue Caves and Shipwreck Beach, and also where car ferries depart for Pessada on Kefalonia. The village sand-and-pebble beach is only a few hundred feet long and is a nice place to sit with a view of the offshore island.

Four kilometres to the north is the extraordinary Cape Skinari, its cliffs home to great tavernas and hiking trails. Here, there are also excursion boats to the caves and Shipwreck Beach at reasonable prices (☛ *Caves tour 10 euros, Caves & Shipwreck Beach 20 euros | potamitisbros.gr). ⚏ D15*

7 BLUE CAVES (GALAZIA SPILEA) ★

The Blue Caves of Zakynthos are every bit as beautiful as their namesakes in Capri. You enter by boat, gliding through natural rock portals and bizarre formations into the crystal-clear, blue and turquoise shimmering water of the caves, where you can swim. Excursion boats to the caves depart regularly from Agios Nikolaos/Skinari and from the pier below the lighthouse at Cape Skinari (this trip has the shortest travel time). There are also boat trips from Zakynthos Town and from Makris Gialos beach. ⚏ D15

8 VOLIMES

The rambling mountain village in the north of the island looks like a large market during the summer. Everywhere along the roadside there are sellers with "genuinely handmade" embroidered cloths and decorated covers. This is a great place for those who are looking for quiet private accommodation. The closest beach is no other than Shipwreck Beach, 4km away (see below). Easier to reach – you can get here by road – is fabulous Porto Vromi, 9.4km to the south (see p. 49). ⚏ D15

9 SHIPWRECK BEACH (NAVAGIO) ★

A 40m-long cargo vessel, which ran aground on the golden-yellow sandy beach here, is a Zakynthos landmark and the second most visited sight in all of Greece – its image is used to promote the country throughout the world. Cigarette smuggling aboard the *MV Panagiotis* ended in dramatic fashion at the foot of this 200m-tall limestone cliff, when the ship ran aground here in 1980. The cove is only accessible by boat. When you come here on a boat trip, you will be able to enjoy a 45-minute swimming break – in the company of lots of other visitors. The water is a strong turquoise, only mixed to a milky hue on certain days when limestone deposits are churned up. The evocative wreck has been oxidising for 40 years and is falling apart.

The best place to take photographs is from the top of the cliffs at the Agios Georgiou Krimnon monastery: continue on the northbound road for 1.2km to the viewpoint (signposted) near the car park. If you walk along the slope towards the Greek flag, you get a better view of the rusting vessel. At the cliff edge, a stone bench and stools have been installed so that it should be easy to get a good shot of both yourself and the scenic panorama. *□ C15*

INSIDER TIP
Perfect selfie spot

⑩ MONASTERY OF AGIOS GEORGIOU KRIMNON

An unusually lively monastery near the steep cliffs in the north-west: behind the walls of this fortified complex you'll find a mighty tower with a Greek flag. Young monks with long hair invite visitors to mass in the Baroque church, even if people are only wearing summer clothes. Liturgical chants emanating from the church can be heard outside on the small terrace. You are offered *lokum* (the Greek version of Turkish delight) to taste. Pots and cutlery clank in the living quarters and cats stretch near

huge flower pots. These impressions will stay with you when you depart towards the Shipwreck viewpoint, 1.5km away. *□ D15–16*

⑪ MONASTERY OF ANAFONITRIA

The uninhabited monastery with a romantic atmosphere on the outskirts of Anafonitria village has its entrance through a massive 15th-century tower gate. The monastery church, with frescoes from the 17th century, is well preserved, and you can see the old oven and olive press used by the monks. The site is cared for by the priest's wife, who clearly has green fingers. The monastery was home to the island saint Dionysios in his last years as abbot. During this time, he demonstrated true Christian brotherly love: he offered asylum to his brother's murderer. The cloisters are freely accessible. *Church May–Sept daily 9am–2pm | admission free | □ D16*

12 PORTO VROMI

A steep road leads to this beach in the north-west, but the slow journey is worth it because the fjord-like double cove, flanked by rock faces, is a dream. If you forgot your parasol, the 10m-long pebble beach has a sundeck and benches. There are several boats in the quay that do excursions out to Shipwreck Beach *(incl. 1 hr swimming break | 20 euros/pers)* | *C–D16*

13 EXO CHORIA

The village of Exo Choria, with its massive ancient olive tree in the village square, lies on the island's circular road. The tree is popular with photographers because of its broad and knarled shape. A visit to the village, with its taverns and small shops, gives you a good idea of rural life on the islands. From here you can also reach over two dozen Venetian cisterns (just 50m away), which are in a field beside the main road towards Volimes. However, they are not as well preserved as those in Agalas. *D16*

14 KAMBI

Kambi is a village that is popular with tourists who come to enjoy the sunset and see the steep cliff with its huge cross. High up on the terrace at one of the tavernas you almost seem to hover above the Ionian Sea. On the left-hand side of the road that leads from the village up to the cross, are some shaft tombs from the Mycenaean period around 1600 BCE (signposted). Over the millennia they have almost become a part of the limestone landscape, so watch out that you don't trip over the stones! *D17*

15 PORTO LIMNIONAS

Getting into the water of the long, narrow fjord-like bay on the west coast is not very easy, so after you have had

Whether you come by boat or car, Porto Vromi's beautiful double cove is worth a visit

your swim you can rest in a deckchair *(8 euros)* or regain your strength at the *Porto Limniona Taverna (€€)* with lovely views out to sea. ⌐⌐ *D17*

16 PORTO ROXA

The seabed is stony and rough in Porto Roxa cove, 2km south of Porto Limnionas. Beach bars and tavernas offer charming sunbeds for free to rest in comfort. A metal jetty allows easy access to the incredibly blue sea. ⌐⌐ *D17*

17 AGALAS

On the west coast, in lush countryside, is the ancient mountain village of Agalas, with its beautiful stone houses. It's worth stopping off at the *Dionysis Art Gallery (irregular opening hours)* which is on the main road towards Kiliomeno.

In the centre of the remote village, a signpost indicates the mile-long way to the Venetian Wells (or *Andronios Wells)*: 11 well-preserved *cisterns* from the Venetian era. They are ideally situated within a valley lined with vineyards *(freely accessible, follow the signs from the village and at the junction continue straight ahead until the tarmac ends)*. These cisterns collected rain water from as early as the 11th century. Today, you can still see your mirror image in the clear waters.

INSIDER TIP
Still waters run deep

Shortly after the north-western end of the village, on the way to the cisterns, on the opposite side of the valley, you will see a cave opening in the rock; you can visit the cave on the

way back. Called *Spileo tou Damianou*, the double-storey cave features numerous stalagmites. ⌐⌐ *E17*

18 LOUCHA 🚩

This village, on the edge of a mountain valley, is inhabited by just a few elderly residents. It escaped damage in the 1953 earthquake and even the newer buildings have done little to change its authentic feel. With its villas with small balconies, and floors and walls made of natural stone, perched between cypress and olive trees, it remains a good example of what Zakynthian villages looked like more than 50 years ago. ⌐⌐ *E16–17*

19 MACHERADO 🚩

The church of *Agia Mavra (daily from sunrise to sunset | admission free)* in the large inland village of Macherado (pop. 950), 8km west of Zakynthos Town, is the most important pilgrimage site on the island. The 16th-century icon of St Mavra, which is covered in a sheath of embossed silver, allegedly has miraculous powers. That's why it has numerous votive plaques around it, each one depicting what the faithful have prayed for: a child, a house, healthy eyes or limbs, a healthy heart and more.

INSIDER TIP
Belief in miracles

Below the village, to the right of the road to Kiliomeno, is the *Panagia Eleftherotria convent (daily 8.30am–noon, 4–7pm)*, home to about 20 nuns. The walls in the outer courtyard are adorned with glittering mosaics

Relax on the beach of Porto Limnionas

and everything is in perfect order – an impression which is confirmed in the well-maintained walled garden and decorated arcades. The convent was founded in 1961 and the abbey church has beautiful frescoes painted in the Byzantine style. In an adjoining room, a nun shows stones from many biblical locations, such as the Sea of Galilee and the house of Mary in Nazareth. The first abbess of the convent gathered them herself on her travels.

From *Grampsas* winery *(April–Oct daily 10am–8pm | ktimagrampsa. gr | approx. 1km from Kalpaki)*, where you can taste local wines and snacks in a beautiful setting *(5–20 euros)*, the surreal looking, white and burgundy-coloured convent is visible once again in the distance. *E17*

20 ARGASSI

Another holiday destination that is popular among British tourists, Argassi stretches along a narrow, sandy beach and the main road on the Skopos Peninsula. Here you find many shops and even more pubs, including the somewhat special *Portokali* bar (p. 55). From here the view of Zakynthos Town is lovely. A *three-arched bridge* from 1805, when the island was under British administration, confirms that Argassi was established well before the days of mass tourism. The ruined bridge is on the beach in front of the *Kamra Beach* resort. *F17*

21 KALAMAKI & LAGANAS

Kalamaki has a sandy beach just as beautiful as that at neighbouring

Olives ripen under the Greek sun

7–10.30pm | historywarmuseum.gr | in the Galaxy Beach Resort | ⏱ 30 mins) shows static tableaux of scenes from wars in Vietnam and Korea, in which Greece took part, as well as World War II.

Some of the beach bars in Laganas have a Cuban theme, but the beaches are so beautiful that there is no need to think of distant lands. 🛏 F17

22 LITHAKIA

Four kilometres north-west of Laganas is this hamlet, with well-preserved farmhouses set among lush green olive trees. It is worth a short stop to visit the 🍃 *Aristeon Olive Press*, with an open-air exhibition, including machinery and botanical infor-

> **INSIDER TIP**
> All about the liquid gold

mation. Two families have been operating the press since 1850. A family member is on hand to explain the long history of the company and the manufacturing process, and you can also enjoy a tasting and purchase some of their organic oil. *Daily 9am–7pm | aristeon.gr | ⏱ 30 mins | 🛏 E–F17*

Laganas, and as you travel along the main road, you notice that both villages almost merge into each other. Here, close to the airport's flight path, tourists like to sunbathe, especially those from the UK, thereby unintentionally endangering the continued existence of the loggerhead turtles. Their egg-laying spots on the beaches are marked with wooden crates, so please don't disturb them.

Both villages have a wide range of daytime and night-time entertainment: restaurants offer Indian food and bars lay on quizzes, karaoke and live sport events on big screens, and sometimes table dancing. The *History War Museum (daily 10am–2.30pm,*

23 KERI

Keri is a picturesque mountain village (pop. 460) in the green south-west that is untouched by tourism. The *Panagia i Keriotissa* church has an impressive Venetian bell tower and a wooden carved iconostasis dating to 1745. From the village centre a road leads 2km to the lighthouse at *Cape Keri*. The view from here over the 100m-high cliff is magnificent. 🛏 E18

24 LIMNI KEROU

Limni Keriou, the 🐦 island's diving centre, 6km from Keri, is worth seeing for the 😋 🐦 *Herodotus Spring*, a source of both water and asphalt-pitch. You can collect some pitch yourself with the sticks provided.

INSIDER TIP
Treasure hunt

Somewhere near the pitch spring a geocache has been hidden *(geocaching.com)*. It's worth trying your luck!

The short pebble beach here is good for swimming, and boats in the harbour will take you on a tour of the *Keri sea caves* on the west side of the island. You can also hire a motor boat – no need for a licence – and set off to explore the steep coastline on your own. ⌘ E–F18

EATING & DRINKING

ALESTA

The atmosphere on St Mark's Square might suggest that you are in Italy! The pizzas at the Alesta restaurant are delicious and the service lives up to the same excellent standards. *Zakynthos Town | Platia Ag. Markou | €€ | ⌘ F17*

FIORO TOU LEVANTE ⛱

The restaurant directly behind the cemetery is worth visiting for its panoramic views. Order a large pizza for two and a salad, and enjoy the scenery. *Ano Gerakari | by the church on the summit | €€ | ⌘ E16*

KOMIS 🚩

Probably the island's prettiest fish taverna is situated at the entrance to the

MORE THAN A THOUSAND NESTS

Loggerhead turtles *(Caretta caretta)* have been digging their nests on the sandy beaches of the Bay of Laganas since time immemorial. From June to August they come ashore in the evening to lay up to 120 ping pong ball-sized eggs before covering them with sand and heading back to the sea. A turtle can lay eggs up to three times during this period. After about 60 days the offspring hatch – again at night – and then immediately make their way to the sea. They orientate themselves by the moonlight reflected on the water.

However, tourism threatens the turtles in various ways. Parasols stuck into the sand can destroy eggs; nocturnal activities on the beach can prevent the mothers from coming ashore to lay their eggs. Statistically, only one in 1,000 hatchlings survives to adulthood. However, everybody can protect nests and hatchlings by treating marked nests with respect. The hatchlings must reach the water alone and without any well-meant help from people. Stay off the beaches at night, avoid using plastic bags and take your rubbish home. For information visit archelon.gr.

Shop and feast in Zakynthos Town's pedestrian zone

ferry pier. An acolyte of the slow food movement, the restaurant has a menu dominated by a variety of freshly caught fish (steak is also available). Starters include the traditional broadbean fava dip and Zakynthian olives. *Zakynthos Town | by the ferry pier | komis-tavern.gr | €€–€€€ | ▥ F16–17*

MATRAKIA
The early bird catches the worm – or in this case the fish. This is what happens in this family-run restaurant, hidden away in a corner. The young proprietors have created a colourful fish taverna with fair prices and beautiful views of the sea and a small island. *Agios Nikolaos | south end of Matrakia Beach | FB: Madrakia Tavern snack-cafe | €€ | ▥ D15*

THE OLD WINDMILL
Panos and his sister, who is also the head chef, have taken the restaurant over from their parents and done a great job at updating it with Athens flair. Not only do you get to enjoy great views from the veranda, but the style and the cuisine are a contemporary mélange of traditional Greek, Middle Eastern and restrained urban bohemia. *Volimes | near Askos animal park | €€ | ▥ D15*

PALII ALITZERINI
The village of Kiliomenos, known for its old houses with courtyards, a church with Gothic elements and an imposing bell tower, has another attraction. The taverna, in a traditional two-storey Zakynthian farmhouse

dating from 1860, is well known by island locals. The ingredients change daily so there is no menu, and the house wine comes from its own vineyard. Occasionally, *kantades* are played in the evening. *June–Sept daily from 7pm, otherwise Fri–Sun from 7pm | Kiliomenos | on the road between campanile and church | €€–€€€ | ⊞ E17*

PORTOKALI

The most unusual restaurant on the island invites you to drinks as well as extensive meals under the motto *polichoros gefson* ("manifold taste experiences"). The colourful decor is as unusual as the menu. The walls are often decorated with contemporary art and there are occasional live concerts and guest appearances by British DJs. *Argassi | main road towards Zakynthos Town | portokalion.gr | €€ | ⊞ F17*

TO KANTOÚNI 🚩 🐖

Sakis Zougras's mother cooks seven dishes each day, including a vegetarian option. Generous

INSIDER TIP
Follow the locals

servings mean the restaurant is popular at lunchtime with local people who know where the food is good. *Zakynthos Town | side road from the harbour promenade, Ag. I Logotheton 15 | € | ⊞ F17*

TO PETRINO 🚩

Above Makris Gialos Beach, this taverna and garden is run by a Swiss family. It offers refined Greek cuisine with regional ingredients in a cosy atmosphere. Home-made oil and wine plus suites to rent next door. *Makris Gialos Beach | makrisgialos.gr | €€ | ⊞ D15*

ELLINON GEFSIS 🚩

The attractively decorated "Greek taste" shop offers culinary delights and cosmetics from all over the country, including numerous organically grown products. *Zakynthos Town | Odos Alex. Roma 13 | ⊞ F16-17*

HANNE MI'S CERAMIC ART STUDIO 🌲

The Norwegian artist Hanne Mi produces ceramics and earthenware of high quality: tiles and fountains, bowls and vases, cups, plates, frames – and, of course, decorative turtles. She also offers a summer academy and pottery classes *(Tue, Fri 10am-noon | 40 euros)* and private lessons *(60 euros). Vassilikos | main road before the turn-off to Porto Roma Beach | ceramichannemi.com | ⊞ G17*

HELMI & CO 🚩

Greek fashion is not internationally known. Helmi is a label that creates pieces like trendy summer dresses at reasonable prices. Everything else that is required for an outfit is also made in Greece. *Zakynthos Town | Odos Alex. Roma 99 | ⊞ F16-17*

LEVANTE BEER 🚩

The hip craft beer from this microbrewery – open to visitors – is a newcomer that has become increasingly popular in the island's restaurants. *Road* between Katastari & Korithi, 1km from Makris Gialos Beach | by appointment only | tel. 69 81 18 97 99 | levante beer.com | ⌗ D15

NOUGAT FACTORY

This is a small factory outlet with roasted almonds, soft Ionian mandolato nougat, pasteli and sesame seed bars, all straight from the manufacturer: guaranteed fresh and well priced. *Panagoulas 14 | west of the main road between Zakynthos Town & Argassi | ⌗ F17*

WINERIES 🚩 🐂

INSIDER TIP
Immediate enjoyment
You will struggle to find Zakynthian wines at home, but you can taste them directly on site in the island's vineyards at great prices. Tasting and tours of the manufacturing facilities are offered by family-run winery *Grampsas (April–Oct daily 10am–8pm | 5–20 euros | ktimagrampsa.gr | Lagopodo, 1km east of Panagia Eleftherotria convent | ⌗ E17),* including snacks in the garden and a tour of the grounds.

More exclusive is wine grower Goumas at *Art & Wine (daily 9am–9pm | 5 euros | artandwine.gr | Goumas Estate, near Orthonies | ⌗ E16),* with its renovated stone buildings, small bar and contemporary art exhibition.

Callinico winery *(Mon-Sat 9am-8pm | Kalipado | signposted from Zakynthos Town | ⌗ F16)* has a museum with historic machinery. It is the ideal place to buy cheaper wines.

ASKOS STONEPARK 👥

Scenically situated between hills in the north of the island, Askos Stonepark is home to deer, African sheep and goats, racoons, lizards and many more animals. There are also local plants, fruit trees, ancient cisterns and a stone wine press to discover. *Askos | May-Sept daily 9am-7pm, Oct-April daily 10am-5pm | admission 8 euros, children aged 5-12 6 euros | http://www.askosstone park.gr | ◷ 1 hr | ⌗ D15*

CARETTA FUNPARK 👥 🐂

A small theme park makes a change from the daily trip to the beach. At the Caretta fun park in Kalamaki, children can let off steam on the bouncy castle and race each other in go-karts while a snack bar provides sustenance. *Kalamaki | Caretta Beach Holiday Village | admission free | carettabeach. com | ◷ 1 hr | ⌗ F17*

MINI GOLF 👥

Two of the most idiosyncratic miniature golf courses in Europe are the work of one local. The two 18-hole courses include replicas of the Golden Gate Bridge, Stonehenge, the Statue of Liberty and many other world-famous landmarks. In the evening, the courses are attractively lit. *Argassi | daily 10am-2am | admission 6 euros | FB: World Tour mini golf | ◷ 1 hr | ⌗ F17*

MOTOR BOATS ⚑

If you rent a motor boat (no licence required) in *Limni Keriou*, you can cross the Bay of Laganas or circle the turtle island of Marathonisi. If you decide to set sail on your own from *Agios Nikolaos*, you can even visit the Blue Caves or the Shipwreck Beach – provided calm seas are forecast.

MOUNTAIN BIKING & HIKING

Bicycle rentals and guided mountain bike tours are offered by *Podilatadiko (tour from 45 euros | tel. 26 95 02 44 34 | podilatadiko.com | Zakynthos Town | Platia Agiou Pavlou/Odos Koutouzi 88)*. The longest tour is 120km around the island, the most strenuous is a 35km-long crossing of the island's mountains. Guided hikes

can also be arranged. Dates and prices are subject to demand and the number of participants.

BEACHES

Numerous beaches line the south and east coast of the island. On the north and west coast, on the other hand, there are only a few exclusive beaches, and almost all of them are only accessible by boat.

BANANA BEACH 🌴

On the Skopos Peninsula this long, dead-straight sandy beach is well-equipped with a first-aid station and wheelchair access. There are sun loungers under palm-thatched parasols and sweepings views over the sea

Levante Beer has introduced Zakynthos to craft beer

Meet the turtles on Gerakas Beach

to the Peloponnese. Food and drink is served at one of the largest *beach bars* in western Greece. Chill out in the hammocks or deckchairs in the shade of the trees (approx. 7–20 euros). *Buses from Argassi & Zakynthos Town stop on the main road 300m from the beach | ᗢ G17*

GERAKAS BEACH 🐢

This scenically beautiful, sandy beach is where sea turtles and tourists try to coexist, which is why there is no beach bar. To the left, the sandstone promontory reaches out to the sea in spectacular fashion, and in one place the rocks have collapsed. Beach use is only allowed during the day and conservationists inform tourists about the correct behaviour. There are a few nice tavernas (without sea views) in the hinterland, which is behind the informative 🐢 *Sea Turtle Information Center (daily 9am–8pm | admission free | earth-sea-sky-global.org | Gerakas, Vasilikos). ᗢ G17–18*

KAMINIA BEACH

The rough sand and fine gravel beach, about 130m long, is backed by some tamarisk trees that provide welcome shade. Sun loungers and umbrellas are available on the green lawn and are provided for free to beach bar guests. There are even some porch swings. *Buses stop on the main road 200m from the beach | ⊞ G17*

MAKRIS GIALOS BEACH ★

Well-maintained gravel beach about 800m south of the scenic hamlet of *Mikro Nisi*, which is built in an idyllic location on a flat ledge that protrudes into the sea. ⊞ D15

SAN NICOLAS BEACH

A 300m-long sandy beach on Skopos Peninsula that has sun lounger rentals, a beach bar, showers, water sports (there's a dive centre) and a great atmosphere. In the north, the beach is bordered by the *St Nicholas chapel* on a low, rocky promontory, which is rather romantic at dusk. ⊞ G17

XIGIA BEACH

Xigia Beach promises an adventurous day by the sea thanks to its special *cantina*. After leaving your car on the top, it's a steep climb down to the beach. Before finding a spot to sunbathe, swim inside the tiny rocky bay, where the bright blue water from the cooling sulphur springs splashes against two tiny coves. This healing water is supposedly good for your complexion and, depending on the current, flows into the bay and sometimes far out to sea. Are you hungry now? Order a snack at the counter on the beach and it will be wheeled down to you in a small wicker basket from the *cantina* at the top. *On the main road around the island | ⊞ E15*

INSIDER TIP
Natural healing spa

WELLNESS

DANCE

Turn your body into an instrument: traditional folk dances allow you to immerse yourself in Ionian culture. Classes are run by Beate Knapp and her team of dance therapists in the courtyard of her bungalow resort ⚑ *Beatehouses* in Agios Sostis *(from July, book in advance | beatehouses.gr | ⊞ F17)*, an enclave close to noisy Laganas.

YOGA

In the middle of an olive grove above Porto Roma Beach, *Daphnes (daphneszakynthos.com | Vasilikos | ⊞ F16)* offers yoga retreats, as well as yoga classes on Wednesdays run by teacher Loukia Pikis. If all the beaches are overrun in summer, you can still find an oasis of peace here. Book in advance.

NIGHTLIFE

111

The cocktail bar in the garden and the traditional stone building behind the *Zakanthi* taverna *(€–€€)* often hosts a DJ. Cocktails are cheap and the party goes on until late at night. *Kalamaki | main road | FB: 111 cocktail bar & more | € | ⊞ F17*

34

Zakynthos has its own alternative culture scene; its meeting place is this café-bar which also serves warm snacks. The bar, in an alleyway in the town centre, attracts a crowd of left-leaning alternative individuals who like to come here with their families to play cards and board games. There's occasional live music along with informative evening events on, for example, refugee issues. *Zakynthos Town | Odos Filita 34 | € | ⊞ F16*

BARRAGE CLUB
Voted into the top ten of the world's best dance clubs by a British magazine, this is *the* club, with a garden bar on the island capital's southern promenade. Regular house parties and pop concerts at maximum sound levels. *Zakynthos Town | on the road south direction Argassi | barrageclub. com | ⊞ F17*

BLISS ART CAFE BAR
While the interior is inspired by modern art, the musical style is jazz. This bar is great because of its central location in the arcades of the pedestrian zone. Very cosy in the late evening. *Zakynthos Town | Odos 25is Martiou 23 | € | ⊞ F16*

MAHOGANI ART CAFE
There are snacks, good drinks and live classical music (including piano) on the stone building's terrace with sea views.

INSIDER TIP
Changing art exhibitions

Changing art exhibitions are held in this Goa trance-style café. *Varvara | on the main road 700m south of Agios Nikolaos | daily from 5pm | €€ | ⊞ D15*

O ADELFOS TU KOSTA ⚑
An idyllically situated garden taverna

where *kantades* are sung in the evenings at weekends; the taverna is known throughout the country for its music. Specialities of the house are rabbit and *kokoras ragu*, a chicken and vegetable stew. *Main road between Banana Beach & Ionion Beach | adelfos toukosta.com | €€ | ⊞ G17*

SARAKINA ⚑
Traditional and touristy at the same time: costumed locals perform Greek dances and sing *kantades* every evening from 7pm to 9pm in the large taverna next to the ruins of the historic manor of Sarakina. The event even ends with a Greek party where you can

dance along. Guests are served Greek dishes and plenty of wine or spirits. A free minibus shuttles between the restaurant and various stops in Laganas from 6.30pm to 10pm. *2km from the centre of Laganas on the road to Pantokratoras, clearly signposted | tel. 26 95 05 16 06 | €€ | 🕮 F17*

VARKAROLA ★ 🚩
Almost every evening from 9pm young musicians perform on Anatolian instruments in the Amanatidis family's taverna next to the harbour promenade. There is a good mixture of local and international folk songs. There's a lovely and easy atmosphere and it's a popular spot: book a table in advance to be immersed in the melodies. *Zakynthos Town | Odos Lomvardou 30 | €€ | 🕮 F16-17*

> **INSIDER TIP**
> Book early to avoid disappointment

TRAVEL

FERRY CONNECTIONS
All-year-round car ferries travel several times daily between Zakynthos Town and Killini (Peloponnese). From May until October a car ferry travels at least twice daily between Agios Nikolaos/Skinari and Pessada (Kefalonia). *levanteferries.com*

Ferry hop to the next dream island!

KEFALONIA

Kefalonia (pop. 36,000) is the biggest island in the Ionian Sea. It covers an area of 786km² meaning that you will not have to lie like sardines on the sublime beaches of Mirtos, Xi or Antisamos.

You can stroll easily through the pretty island capital of Argostoli, or through Assos and Fiskardo in the elegant north of the island, with their small coves for yachts and bathing. Pleasant holiday villages with water sports options and a peaceful atmosphere can be found in

The north coast of Kefalonia offers small pockets of beach paradise

the south in charming Metaxata, with its 1950s villas. In the island's interior, you will encounter the magical caves of Drogarati and Melissani, as well as spectacular mountain views on hikes up Agia Dinami and Mount Ainos. Both flora and fauna are varied, with plants (which we know as indoor specimens in cooler countries) that can easily reach heights of two metres. While seismic stress always lurks under the island's surface – the 1953 earthquake caused considerable damage – your own tension will tangibly decrease. Time to let go.

KEFALONIA

MARCO POLO HIGHLIGHTS

★ **ARGOSTOLI**
Mediterranean island town by a lagoon, with ample space for strolling ➤ p. 66

★ **MONASTERY OF AGIOS GERASIMOS**
A pilgrimage destination in deserted heights near a Robola winery ➤ p. 68

★ **MELISSANI CAVE**
View stalagmites and stalactites from a rowing boat ➤ p. 71

★ **ASSOS**
A small coastal village, a mighty fortress with beautiful views and a pebble beach ➤ p. 71

★ **FISKARDO**
Small village with a picturesque harbour straight from a storybook ➤ p. 72

★ **MIRTOS BEACH**
Apart from the crashing of waves, there is nothing to distract your attention from the beauty of this wide sandy beach nestled between steep cliffs ➤ p. 77

★ **PALIKI PENINSULA**
Red sandy beaches below dazzling white chalk cliffs whose clay is great for facials ➤ p. 77

Ormos Athera

Ormos Mirtos

Αθέρας
Atheras

Αγκώνα
Agkona

○ **Paliki Peninsula ★**

Ormos Pethani

Καρδακάτ
Kardakata

🏖 Petani Beach

Λιβάδι
Livadi

Κοντογενάδα
Kontogenada

Φάρσα
Fársa

Καμιναράτα
Kaminarata

Ormos Argostoliou

20 mins

16 ◄ Lixouri

Χαβριάτα
Chavriata

🏖 Xï Beach

Argostoli ★ 1

Lassi Peninsula 2

Cephalon Botani

8km, 35 mins

Ι Ο Ν Ι Ο
Π Ε Λ Α Γ Ο Σ
Ι Ο Ν Ι Ο
P E L A G O S

Ormos Vatsa

5 km
3.11 mi

Όρμος Αρφαλές
Ormos Arfales

☀ ⛱ Emblisi Beach
Μάγγανος
Maganos
15 Fiskardo ★
Σταυρός
Stavros
Κιόνι
Kioni

Ανωγή
Anogi

Βασιλικιάδες
Vasilikiades

Λεύκη
Lefki

14 Assos ★
Αγία Σοφία
Agia Sofia

Βαθύ
Vathý

Κομιτάτα
Komitata

⛱ Mirtos Beach ★
Διβαράτα
Divarata

Περαχώρι
Perahori

Αγία Ευφημία
Agia Efimia

Όρμος Σάμης
Ormos Samis

🚗

☀ ⛱ Antisamos

Melissani Cave ★ 13
12
Καραβόμυλος
Karavomilos
11 Sami

Όρμος Κουτσουπιά
Ormos Koutsoupia

10 Drogarati Cave
Χαλιωτάτα
Chaliotata

ΕΛΛΑΣ
GREECE

Διγαλέτο
Digaleto

Τρωιανάτα
Troianata

6 Monastery of Agios Gerasimos ★

Όρμος Πόρου
Ormos Porou

9 Poros

4 Kastro Agiou Georgiou

Μουσάτα
Mousata

7 Mt Ainos

Τζανάτα
Tzanata

Όρμος Γονιές
Ormos Gonies

Μεταξάτα/
Κουρκουμελάτα
Metaxata/
Kourkoumelata

Πεσάδα
Pesada

Σιμωτάτα
Simotata

Πάστρα
Pastra

Όρμος Λούρδα
Ormos Lourda

Βαλεριάνος
Valerianos

8 Skala

Όρμος Αβύθος
Ormos Avithos

Όρμος Κατελιού
Ormos Kateliou

Κάτω Κατελειός
Kato Katelios

34km, 45 mins
19km, 25 mins
71km, 1 hr 40 mins

SIGHTSEEING

1 ARGOSTOLI ★

On the Lassi Peninsula, Argostoli (pop. 9,000) is the island's capital, founded by the Venetians in 1757. The elegant town doesn't look out across the open sea but onto a lagoon which opens into the ocean. The town centre is linked with the island's interior by the *De Bosset Bridge*. At almost 690m, it features in the Guinness Book of World Records as the longest stone bridge across the sea. Strolling along it, with its historic lanterns, you will come upon a pretty obelisk that seems to float on the water. This is a reminder of the British, who ruled the island in the 19th century.

There was little of substance in the town that was able to withstand

Today the temple on the Lassi Peninsula is an oasis of peace by the open sea

the earthquake of 1953: this is documented in the *Earthquake 1953* photographic exhibition, at the *Cosmetatos Foundation (May–Oct Mon–Fri 10am–2pm | admission 5 euros (combined ticket with the Botanical Garden, see p.67) | Platia Vallianou |* ⏱ *30 mins)*. The rebuilding work created a small Mediterranean metropolis with wide squares, pedestrian zones and a shoreline promenade with tavernas, bars and delicatessens, while yachts moor in the harbour. In the south of the town the 🐖 market creates a lively atmosphere during the day, and fish are sold every morning 100m further down the pier.

Minimalist and temple-like: the impressive building of the *Korgialenios Library* gives local readers access to more than 60,000 books. At the *Historic and Cultural Museum (Mon–Sat 9am–2pm | admission 3 euros | Ilia Servou 12 |* ⏱ *45 mins)* visitors can learn about the historic clothing, art and crafts of the region, both aristocratic and rural.

The *Agios Spiridonis* church is on the main shopping street, *Lithostrato*. The interior was completely painted with Byzantine-style frescoes during the 1970s. The evening *volta* (stroll), which seems to get the entire town on their feet, takes place between the *Platia Vallianou* and the 1960s building of the courthouse and town theatre of *O Kefalos (Leoforos Vergoti Georgiou)*, where children play outside until late in the evening and sometimes small-scale 🐖 concerts with Greek music are held on warm summer evenings. At the *Radio Museum (daily 10am-9pm | admission 4.50 euros | Chamber of Commerce | Leoforos Vergoti Georgiou 131 | ⏱ 45 mins)*, Haris Makris displays a fascinating collection of transmitters and receivers from across the globe. *B11-12*

2 LASSI PENINSULA

The Lassi Peninsula, which protrudes into the bay between the main island and the Paliki (Lixouri) Peninsula, is easily circumnavigated on foot or by bicycle. To the north of the town, behind the ferry port (where you can cross over to Lixouri), at the end of a small wood, a historic seawater mill has been carefully restored. This water mill is on the premises of the trendy *Katavothres* lounge restaurant *(daily | Mikeli Davi 10 | €€-€€€)*, which turns into a club in the evening. In 1820, the British built a small *round temple* in the Doric style on the headland, which served as a beacon at the harbour entrance. Some 800m further on, a signposted road branches off the

coastal road and leads 700m to the *Monumento Caduti (freely accessible | divisioneacqui.com)*. The memorial commemorates the 9,470 Italian soldiers, who after Italy's defeat in September 1942 refused to surrender to German troops and were consequently killed. The town's beach at *Makris Gialos*, 4km to the south, is good for bathing. *B11-12*

3 CEPHALONIA BOTANICA

Kefalonia is green even in the heat of the summer, and the botanical garden on the edge of the town, which is taken care of by a local foundation, is equally lush. Indigenous plants flourish between modern sculptures in the well-maintained park, with koi carp in the rose pond. Let your senses be revived in the herb pavilion, with Mediterranean scents of thyme and sage! *Argostoli | southern edge of town, signposted | May-Oct Mon-Sat 9am-2pm | admission 5 euros (combined ticket with*

INSIDER TIP
There's a herb for everything

WATER FLOWING INLAND

Why does seawater get sucked inland and flow into the swallow holes on the Lassi Peninsula? And where does it go? The answer to these questions remained a mystery for a long time, but this natural phenomenon was used to power seawater mills until 1953. Two of these water mills have been preserved, one of which is now the lounge restaurant and club in Argostoli (Katavothres, see above left). Austrian geologists once had the clever idea of pouring green dye into the seawater at Argostoli. Several days later it appeared in the cave of Melissani right over the other side of the island (see p. 71). The lake's amazing colours are now completely natural again.

the Earthquake 1953 exhibition, see p.66 | focascosmetatos.gr | ⌐ B12

4 KASTRO AGIOU GEORGIOU 🐷

The Livatho plain is dominated by the 320m-high mountain ridge where the island capital of Agios Georgios was located until 1757. The air is filled with a strong scent of oregano. Today its Venetian castle, the *Kastro*, with around 600m of walls, is surrounded by a quiet little village, whose cafés and tavernas have wonderful views over the island from their terraces. *May–Oct Wed–Mon 8.30am–4pm | admission 3 euros | to the left above the road from Argostoli to Skala |* ⌐ C12

5 METAXATA/ KOURKOUMELATA 🚩

These two villages in the island's south (Livatho district), which merge seamlessly with each other, were destroyed by the 1953 earthquake. The Vergottis shipping family supported them after the catastrophe with generous donations, and many attractive new houses were built. The round shapes of the red, white, blue and yellow villas are reminiscent of American suburbs of the 1950s, but they were actually built according to a Swiss model, and were intended to create the "most perfect village in Europe". Today, the gardens and streets on the commanding hillside are still carefully maintained, making for a pleasant short stroll. Afterwards, enjoy a piece of *pasta flora* (jam tart) in the ship-shaped Café Marina *(FB: Marina Cafe | Kourkoumelata | €–€€)*.

Outside the village, heading north, are fenced but accessible shaft and chamber tombs from the late Mycenaean era *(Argostoli-Pessada road, shortly before the turn off to Metaxata, at Mazarakata, opposite the sign)*. ⌐ C12

6 MONASTERY OF AGIOS GERASIMOS ★ ☂

The most visited monastery on the island stands on the edge of the Omalon plain, 400m above sea level and surrounded by mountains. In this region, the famous Robola wine grape is cultivated and pressed in the cellars of an independent winegrower near the monastery, *Orealios Gaia (guided tour & wine tasting daily 9am–3pm, booking recommended | robola.gr)*.

The monastery grounds are as well maintained as the monastery itself. You can stroll through the magical park and admire a 500-year-old plane tree. At the entrance to the old church, nuns point out the cloaks to be worn inside to cover shoulders and knees (hire fee applicable). The bones of the saint rest in a coffin and can be kissed by pilgrims through two small openings. A trapdoor in the church floor leads down a steep ladder into a cave where the island's saint once lived for a time. *April–Oct daily 3.30am–1pm, 3.30–8pm, Nov–March 4am–1pm, 3–7pm | access signposted along the Argostoli–Sami road |* ⌐ C12

7 MOUNT AINOS

You can drive on a 15-km paved road up to the summit area of the highest mountain in the Ionian

After a visit to the Agios Gerasimos monastery, head for the hilly Robola vineyards

Islands. The 23-km² area has been turned into a national park. There are several nice picnic spots along the moderate park trail as well as wild flowers, wild animals and Kefalonia fir trees, which don't grow anywhere else on Earth. The conservation of this unique area of pine forest is particularly important. A 2-km circular trail takes you around the peak, starting from the forest. The view is particularly interesting for those who have flown from Zakynthos to Kefalonia as you can see both airports from up here, provided there is no fog. *Signposted turn-off on the Argostoli–Sami road* | ▢ D12

8 SKALA

At the southern end of the small seaside resort (pop. 550) – where visitors relax on the long sandy beach or in beach bars and cafés, or take part in all kinds of water sports *(dolphinskiclub-kefalonia.weebly.com)* – are the well-preserved foundations of a *Roman villa (Mon–Fri 8.30am–3.30pm | admission free)*. A protective roof shelters two well-preserved floor mosaics: one depicts the sacrifice of three animals and the other one a young man who symbolises envy.

There is even more Roman history towards the north where, opposite a chapel, a few stones mark the site of a Roman temple in a prime beachfront location. ▢ E13

9 POROS

The harbour village (pop. 900) spreads over two coves. The place is important in terms of transport because the ferries for Killini (in the Peloponnese) depart from here. About 500m above the village and 6km on foot is the

Boating on the blue and green lake in front of the Melissani Cave

oldest monastery on the island, *Moni tis Iperagias Theotokou Atrou (access: just under a mile from the shore, the road branches off after a ravine on the Poros–Argostoli road).* The first written evidence of it dates back to 1264. Behind the modern building, where the monks now live, the old monastery and chapels rise up amid magnificent mountain scenery, with superb views of the coast and the Peloponnese.

A mere 3km inland, shortly before Tzanata, is a Mycenaean *tholos tomb (daily except Tue 8.30am–4pm | admission 3 euros | brown sign pointing to Tzanata)* from around 1350 BCE. It was constructed on the site of an even older cemetery dating from 1600 BCE. You enter via terraces on which a garden has been created – like a mini-palace. *III E12*

🔟 DROGARATI CAVE 🌂

When the sun is high in the sky, it can be nice to cool down to 18°C. You climb 44m down into the stalactite-filled cave. At the bottom, the carefully illuminated space opens up to a hall with incredible acoustics. Concerts are held here occasionally and world-renowned soprano Maria Callas even performed here once. *Daily 9am–4pm | admission 4 euros | Haliotata | road from Argostoli to Sami (3km away) | III C11*

🔟 SAMI

Sami (pop. 1,100) stretches out at the foot of a mountain, where the ancient city walls are still plainly visible. In the town itself there are the 5m-high brick walls of a preserved *Roman bath*, otherwise you will find various cafés and tavernas on the promenade. A long,

where you have breathtaking views of Ithaca. *D11*

⑫ KARAVOMILOS 😷

The village was rebuilt after the 1953 earthquake and a small lake was created between the sea and the houses. It's filled with a unique mixture of fresh water and seawater, with the latter being sucked into the lake bed through underground channels from the west of the island. The water flows along a short channel into the Gulf of Sami; a restored waterwheel at a former flour mill was once fed by its water. The waterwheel now stands on the site of the *Karavomilos* taverna (*on the road from Agia Efimia to Sami | tavernakaravomilos.com | €) C–D11*

narrow sandy beach stretches from Sami almost to Karavomilos.

To reach the archaeological ruins of the fortified settlement of *Ancient Sami*, first follow the signposted road at the north-eastern edge of the village uphill to the *Monastery of Agrilion*, and then follow the city walls. At *Agioi Fanentes*, a medieval monastery, the walls almost touch the dirt road. Some parts of the building's external walls are still standing while others have been propped up with wooden beams. Next to them you can have a little rest on the steps of a chapel. Continuing past a free-standing bell on a wooden rack, it is another five minutes walk to the ruins of the medieval church of *Agios Nikolaos*, from

INSIDER TIP
Ghost town in the pine woods

⑬ MELISSANI CAVE ★

A visit by boat to this stalactite-filled cave, which has been used by humans for 20,000 years and is known as the "cave of the nymphs", is a special experience. This is especially true in the afternoon as the sunlight is perfect then, filtering through an opening which is framed by green trees and making the cave's crystal-clear water shimmer in hues of blue and green. At the back of the cave, the water laps a small islet where there was a sanctuary to the god Pan in the ancient world. *Daily 10am–4pm | admission 6 euros | 2km from Sami | C10*

⑭ ASSOS ★

The village of Assos (pop. 100), with its pastel-painted façades, lies at the inner end of a sheltered bay that is popular with sailors. On Paris Square

Fish in Fiskardo: one of the prettiest places to eat on the Ionian Islands

land is covered in olive groves, and there are more ruins to discover. The recently renovated former prison has already begun to slowly decay – yet again. *C9*

C9

🔟 FISKARDO ★

The most beautiful (and expensive) village on the island is on the curving shoreline of a small bay opposite Ithaca, and it exudes an air of luxury. The old, well-kept houses along the quay are the ideal backdrop for the lively hustle and bustle on the short waterfront; elegant yachts and small ferry boats fill the port. An exquisite selection of merchandise, good tavernas and boutique hotels have made this village an exclusive destination. At the end of the shoreline, on the upper floor of the *Aiolos* crafts and souvenir shop is an *exhibition (promenade | admission 2.5 euros incl. olive soap | ⏱ 30 mins)* of black-and-white photographs and tools used for the olive harvest and fishing in Fiskardo. On the west side of the village's southern bay you find the ruins of a Roman cemetery.

The village was named after the Norman ruler Robert Guiscard, who died here in 1085. The *Norman church* (accessible on foot) on the peninsula north of the port's bay was built in his honour. For bathing there is the gorgeous 🏖 *Emblisi Beach* 2km further north. *C8*

you can find a nice place to sit in the *Platanos* taverna *(€€)*. The east of the village is bordered by terraced slopes, and on the west side is a peninsula with the remains of a late 16th-century *Venetian fortress (freely accessible during the day, car park on the isthmus which connects the village with the peninsula)*. The Venetians managed the north of the island from Assos. The roughly mile-long ascent to the fortress is on slate rubble and every bend brings wonderful views of the picturesque village. On the top, behind the imposing gate, the castle ruins sit amid overgrown greenery.

Looking out from the fortress, the

C8

🔟 LIXOURI

The main town (pop. 3,500) on the Paliki (or Lixouri) Peninsula was founded in 1534 and still exudes the kind of grace and gentility which most towns on the Ionian Islands lost after the 1953 earthquake. The commercial centre spreads out around the bus station and the social centre is the *platia* on the coastal road. At the end of the coastal road is a white school building in the Bauhaus style. For bar hopping, return to the *platia* parallel to the shoreline on the cobbled Lambraki Street. One of the villas in the upper part of the town today serves as the *Typaldon Iakovaton*, which includes a library. It is currently being restored after a 2014 earthquake and is yet to open to the public. Once the work is finished, you will be able to admire creatively painted ceilings, furniture and many other household items belonging to the wealthy Lakovatios family in the 19th- and 20th-century rooms. There is a frequent, round-the-clock ferry service between Argostoli and Lixouri. *B11*

EATING & DRINKING

AGRAPIDOS ⚑

Inexpensive family-run taverna serving hearty Greek food, with a magnificent view. Wine from their own vineyard, home-made bread, vegetables from their own garden. *Poros | above the harbour on the road to Skala | FB: taverna agrapidos | €–€€ | E12*

AVLI

The menu includes quinoa salad with spinach, pears and basil, as well as the hearty island speciality *kreatopita* – exquisite and creative Greek cuisine by chef Aliki Moschopoulou. There is music for chilling in the airy courtyard. *Lixouri | end of the shoreline road, Lampraki/Ir. Politechniou | FB | €€ | B11*

BEVERINOS ⚑ 🐖

Affordable, authentic *mezedopolio* where you can order snacks to accompany a glass of wine, ouzo or grappa-like schnapps. Popular with young people. They sometimes play rock music. *Argostoli | Odos St. Metaxa 9 | € | B12*

KASTRO

The taverna at the entrance to the Venetian castle is a shady idyll in a sea of flowers. Host Spiros and his wife Niki serve affordable lunches and home-made cakes. *Directly below Kastro Agios Georgios | € | C12*

KIANI AKTI

More than 40 tables are laid out on a wooden platform right above the water at this traditional *ouzeri*. The waiter shows off an appetising display of freshly caught mussels and sea urchins in front of the taverna, and sometimes they serve cooked fish. Excellent service; the seafood is pricey but worth it. *Argostoli | coastal road, at the cruise ship terminal | tel. 26 71 02 66 80 | €€€ | B12*

ROSIE'S KITCHEN BAR

Rosie has created a laid-back oasis in the mountains where the more sophisticated islanders come to dine throughout the year. Herbal tea from the French press and organic egg omelettes are the real favourites. *Karia | main road | €€ | ⌑ C9*

THALASSINO TRIFILLI
Lourdata has a long beach with pubs along the promenade. However, it is nicer to sit further uphill in the cosy taverna garden of Vangelis Dimitratos, who serves vegetarian food, seafood and pizza – prepared with home-made olive oil and organic produce. *Lourdata | main road, 300m before the beach on the right-hand side | €–€€ | ⌑ D12*

TO PATRIKO
The *tsipouradiko* invites you to enjoy a liqueur, but you should first create a solid foundation with hearty dishes such as fish, grilled sausage and cheese, or a bean salad). Listen to live music on colourful chairs under the open sky. *Argostoli | northern shore-line road behind the ferry port, Leof. Antoni Tritsi 28 | €€ | ⌑ B12*

SHOPPING

ROBOLA 🛍
The small shop, named after the famous grape, stocks all the wines from the local cooperative at affordable prices. Decent wines are also sold on tap. *Argostoli | the market | ⌑ B12*

VOSKOPOULA
In this bakery (founded in 1910) you can watch typical Kefalonian sweets being produced. Especially worth trying are the almond and nut delicacies.

Argostoli | Odos Lithostrato 3 | voskopoula.gr | ⌑ B12

WINE
The island's many wine growers focus on the local Robola grape, and some offer tours of their estates and tastings. We recommend a visit to the *Gentilini estate (Minia | road from the airport to Argostoli | gentilini.gr | ⌑ B12)* run by the Kosmetatos family, which has been producing high-quality wine since 1984, using the local Mavrodafni and Robola grapes. On a guided tour you get to know the facilities and can taste their produce.

The *Robola Cooperative (Orealios Gaia | tour & tasting daily 9am–3pm, booking recommended | robola.gr | ⌑ C12)* directly below Mount Ainos near the Agios Gerasimos monastery has a vast estate that is suitable for events.

Estates in the wine-growing villages on the Paliki Peninsula are smaller, which is why you should get in touch before visiting the following: *Foivos (domainefoivos.com), Sclavos Zisimatos (tel. 30 26 71 09 19 30), Haritatos Vineyard (tel. 69 73 44 63 52)*.

Gerasimos Hartouliaris is pleased to welcome visitors to his not particularly commercialised village winery of *Cava Divino (Pessada, village centre | winegarandroses.com | ⌑ C12)*. After your tour of the 1864 building, including an exhibition, you can taste their Retsina and Robola wines as well as rosé and balsamic vinegar.

If you like wine, Kefalonia is a good place to be

SPORT & ACTIVITIES

DONKEY TREKKING

Katharina runs a farm near Sami at *Donkey Trekking Kefalonia (Sami | Grizata 1 | 25 euros/hr | tel. 69 80 05 96 30 | donkeytrekkingkefalonia.com | ▥ D11)*, offering trips with her five animals on ancient trails. If you weigh less than 55kg, you can sit on the donkey's back, while everybody else walks alongside. Treks last between one and eight hours.

FANTASTIC PARK

Daily from 6pm, children can drive small electric jeeps on the permanent fairground Fantastic Park at the northern end of the Odos Rizospaston in Argostoli. There are also remote-control boats – great fun! *FB | ▥ B11*

KAYAKING

Rent a kayak and go out to sea. A variety of day-tours around Kefalonia are offered by *Sea Kayaking Kefalonia (seakayakingkefalonia-greece.com).*

ODYSSEUS ZOO LAND

A mixture of mythology and animal park for families. Miniature buildings and larger-than-life heroes from antiquity go hand in hand with geese, fawns, donkeys and parrots. This is a way to get children interested in Greek mythology! *Main road Argostoli direction Sami, 4km north of the Drogarati cave | admission under-5s free, age 5–12 4 euros | odysseuszooland.com | ▥ D11*

REGIONAL COOKING

At *Chez Vassiliki (Karavados | approx. 65 euros incl. wine & recipes | tel. 69 44 26 68 57 | FB: Chez-Vassiliki | ▥ C12)* the Bali family begin their courses by sending participants into the garden to harvest fresh produce.

Mirtos Beach is cherished by romantics and photographers alike

Then, in a small group, you will learn the tips and tricks of Ionian cuisine, followed by a communal meal.

RIDING
Bavaria Horse Riding Stables (Sami | Koulourata | tel. 69 77 53 32 03 | kephalonia.com | ⊞ D11) and owner Cornelia offer riding programmes and hacks of between one and five hours.

BEACHES

ANTISAMOS ⭐🏖
This 800m-long pebble beach 5km north-east of Sami is best known as the location of numerous scenes from *Captain Corelli's Mandolin*. It is quite undeveloped and surrounded by trees. ⊞ D10

KAMINIA BEACH
Miles of isolated beach in the extreme south of the island opposite Zakynthos offer space even in high season. *Access signposted on the Skala–Ratzakli road* | ⊞ E13

KATELIOS BEACH 🏖
A beach for those who like a waterfront café or taverna to enjoy a refreshing drink in between sunbathing and swimming. Also ideal for non-swimmers and young children as the water remains shallow (around 1m) until quite far out – almost as safe as the non-swimmers' section of the pool at home! ⊞ E13

MAKRIS GIALOS & PLATIS GIALOS
Beautiful sandy beaches with tavernas, lots of water sports activities and sun

lounger rentals. Very popular in summer. On the side of the Lassi Peninsula that faces away from Argostoli. *Hourly bus connections to nearby Argostoli | ᗰ B12*

MIRTOS BEACH ★ *☀

A stunning 1km-long and 100m-wide beach with sand and dazzling white pebbles. The shoreline has been shaped by its longshore drift and high breakers. Before coming here, check the wind and weather because bathing is not always safe. From the viewpoint on the Assos to Argostoli road you can spot whether the sea is calm enough for swimming. A steep winding road leads down the coast to the unspoilt beach with just a small *cantina* and car park at the bottom. ᗰ C9

> **INSIDER TIP**
> **Viewpoint weather forecast**

PALIKI PENINSULA ★

There are many quiet, isolated beaches on the *Paliki (or Lixouri) Peninsula*. Red sand stretches from the low, white cliffs along the entire southern coast of the peninsula. The clay from the 20m- to 30m-high cliffs has traditionally been used by the Greeks for cosmetic facials. *☀ Xi Beach* with its shallow sloping shoreline is particularly beautiful, and *Baywatch Watersports (baywatch kefalonia.gr)* offers kayaking, parasailing, jet-skiing and wakeboarding here. The crescent-shaped *Vatsa Beach*, with a small fishing harbour and the relaxed *Spiaggia Vatsa beach taverna* also has water sports. If you are looking for your dream beach, visit the light-coloured, sandy *☀ Petani Beach* in the west of the peninsula. ᗰ A–B12

NIGHTLIFE

CAJABLANCA CLUB

The place to dance the night away. The "Greek Night" is actually not a folk event, and international hits feature highly on the playlist. For a break, sit down in the adjoining *Via Vallianou* café. *Argostoli | Panagi Vallianou 11 | ᗰ B12*

LIBRETTO

The island's arts café, with its beautiful tiled floor, is focused on ecology. Frequent live music, such as Greek *rembetiko*. *Argostoli | Platia Kambanas (at the clock tower) | ᗰ B12*

TRAVEL

FERRY CONNECTIONS

All year round, several times a day, from Sami to Pisoaetos (Ithaca) and Astakos (mainland). All year round from Poros to Killini/Peloponnese. All year round from Fiskardo to the island of Lefkada (Vassiliki) and from there to Frikes/Ithaca.

From May to October twice daily between Pessada in the south of the island and Agios Nikolaos (Zakynthos).

FLIGHTS

There are direct flights, including with easyJet and Jet2, from UK airports to Kefalonia.

ITHACA

GENTLE & SHROUDED IN LEGEND

Known locally as Thiaki, the small island of Ithaca (pop. 3,200) is said to be the home of Homer's hero Odysseus, and as a result there are numerous places on the island that purport to be linked to *The Odyssey* – often with signs explaining the connection. Even if these connections are mere legend, Ithaca's beautiful scenery often makes the walk to them worthwhile.

Ithaca lies off the eastern coast of Kefalonia, from which it is separated by a narrow strait. The island is 24km long and 6km wide,

Ithaca's main town of Vathi is picturesquely situated in a bay

and its northern and southern parts are connected by a narrow strip of land just 600m wide. On Ithaca, you will find unspoiled nature, lush green forests and crystal-clear water in the island's tiny coves. Life is leisurely in the villages of the hilly north. Similarly, the laid-back main town of Vathi in the south, or the mountain village of Perachori, are for those who want to escape the hustle and bustle and are keen to taste the heavily scented local honey.

Ithaca smells of freedom and thyme: breathe in deeply.

ITHACA

Αντπάτα
Antipata

Φισκάρδο
Fiskardo

Μάγγανος
Maganos

Τσελεντάτα
Tselentata

Ormos
Fiskárdo

Εξωγή
Exogi

Λαχός
Lahos

Ormos
Afales

Κονιδαράτα
Konodarata

Ormos
Doulícha

στενα Ιθάκης
Stena Ithakis

Ormos
Poli

7 Stavrc

Μεσοβούνια
Mesovounia

Δραπανίτικα
Drapanitika

Λεύκη
Lefki

Πλαγιά
Plagia

Ormos
Assou

Δεφαρανάτα
Defaranata

Agios Ioannis Beach

Άσος
Assos

Καρυά
Karya

Αγία Σοφία
Agia Sofia

Ormos
Mirtou

Κομιτάτα
Komitata

Νεοχώρι
Neochori

Διβαράτα
Divarata

Αντιπάτα
Antipata

2 km
1.24 mi

Μακριώτικα
Makriotika

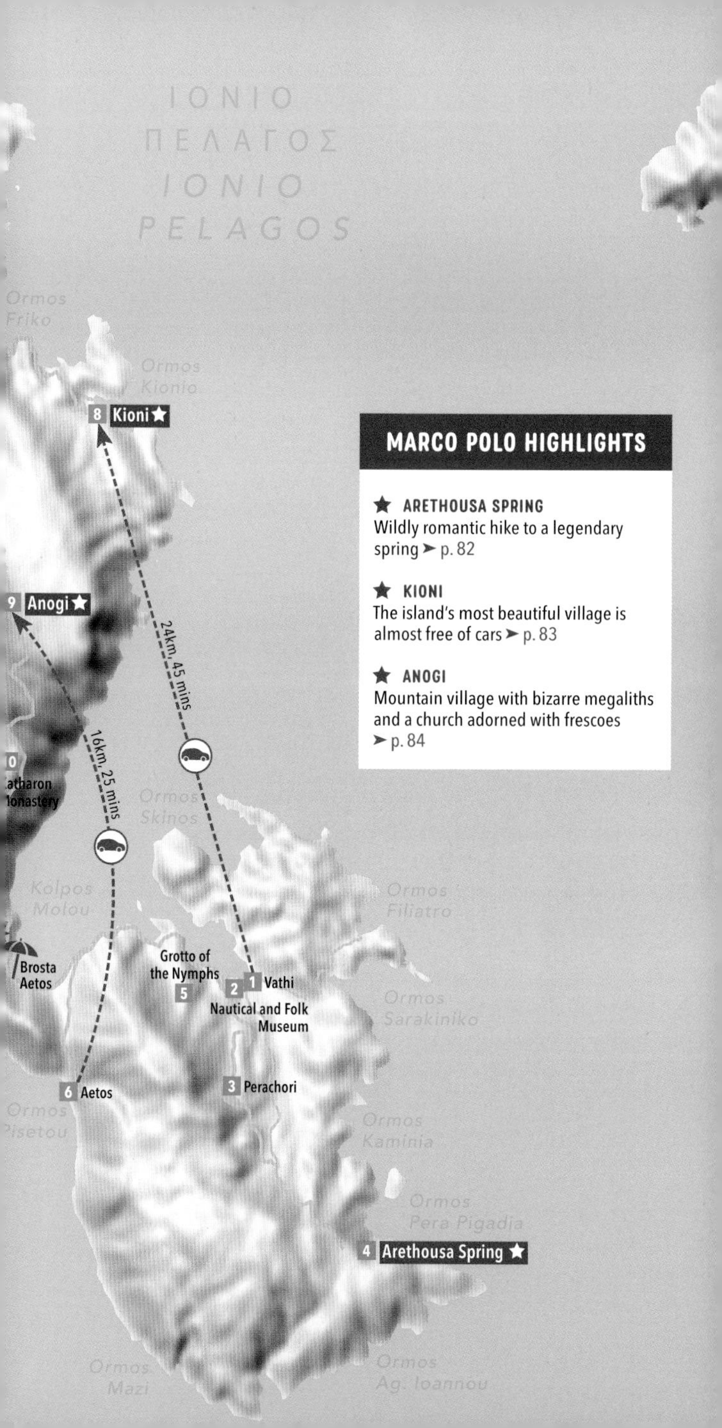

IONIO
ΠΕΛΑΓΟΣ
IONIO
PELAGOS

Ormos Friko

Ormos Kioni

8 Kioni ★

9 Anogi ★

24km, 45 mins

16km, 25 mins

0 athoron Monastery

Ormos Skinos

Kolpos Molou

Brosta Aetos

Grotto of the Nymphs

5 **2** **1 Vathi**

Nautical and Folk Museum

Ormos Filiatro

Ormos Sarakiniko

3 Perachori

6 Aetos

Ormos Pisetou

Ormos Kaminia

Ormos Pera Pigadia

4 Arethousa Spring ★

Ormos Mazi

Ormos Ag. Ioannou

MARCO POLO HIGHLIGHTS

★ **ARETHOUSA SPRING**
Wildly romantic hike to a legendary spring ➤ p. 82

★ **KIONI**
The island's most beautiful village is almost free of cars ➤ p. 83

★ **ANOGI**
Mountain village with bizarre megaliths and a church adorned with frescoes ➤ p. 84

SIGHTSEEING

1 VATHI

The island's capital (pop. 2,000) is a tranquil town with no significant sights. It lies at the inner end of a long fjord-like bay, which winds its way to the sea. It can get quite lively at night in the cafés along the waterfront, a promenade that gives one the feeling of sitting on the shores of a large lake. The elegant Drakoulis Villa, built by an influential local family in the neo-classicist style in 1920, goes well with the dozens of yachts that are moored here. When entering the bay, the yachts pass the islet of *Lazareto* where, in the 15th century, foreigners had to quarantine for up to 40 days before they were allowed to set foot on the island.

INSIDER TIP
Taxi to the beach

You can swim to the islet and excursion boats also make trips to the short shingle beaches on the other side of the bay. *D9*

2 NAUTICAL & FOLK MUSEUM

This is a small, local museum in a converted power station. Because Ithaca has been a seafaring island since the time of Odysseus, many of the displays reference the sea. *Vathi | May–Oct Mon–Sat 9am–1pm, July/ Aug also 6–10pm | admission 3 euros | 45 mins | D9*

3 PERACHORI

Around 3km from Vathi is the island's largest village (pop. 500), built on a hill at a height of 300m. Terraced vineyards and olive groves sit between the houses on the slopes; the view of the harbour bay is extraordinarily beautiful. Several ruins testify to a medieval settlement in the area. You can rent a place to stay here in these beautiful surroundings or enjoy the spectacular views from the café *Veranda sto Ionio (€€)*. Right at the lower village entrance, on the left side of the road, are the remains of a Venetian house and a church, where the remnants of some frescoes can be seen. *D9*

4 ARETHOUSA SPRING ★

A beautiful 50-minute hike leads from Perachori (3km from Vathi) to the spring at the base of a steep rock face on the south-east coast of the island. It is here that Eumaeus, Odysseus's swineherd, brought his master's pigs to drink. From Perachori, follow the "Arethousa Spring" signposts through the village and then continue on the narrow tarmac road until you reach a sign where the narrow footpath down to the spring begins. *E10*

5 GROTTO OF THE NYMPHS

After his successful return to Ithaca, Odysseus left his belongings in the care of the nymphs – mythical creatures that lived in a small cave above Dexia Bay. The ceiling caved in during an earthquake in 373 BCE. *It is dangerous to enter the cave; take a torch to illuminate the inside from the outside!* Today, Dexia Bay is a shingle beach suitable for bathing. *D9*

6 AETOS

Welcome! This is where the ferry from Sami (Kefalonia) and Patra on the

Thousands of years ago, even Odysseus may have longed for the idyllic alleyways of Kioni

mainland arrives. Bathe in the bay of *Piso Aetos* near Pisaetos harbour. The beach of ⭐ *Brosta Aetos* on the other side of the island's narrow isthmus also has shallow water – ideal for non-swimmers. The ancient city Alalkomene was located on the eastern slope of the 380m-high hill southwest of Vathi. It was settled from about 1400 BCE to Roman times. You can reach the ruins on a mile-long hike. On the summit there are some well-preserved cisterns and a part of the wall of the acropolis that dates from the fifth century BCE. *D9*

7 STAVROS

The largest village (pop. 350) in the north of the island is situated on a high ridge, with views of both the east and the west coast of Ithaca. It is an ideal spot for a coffee break, with freshly baked cake in the cafés on the

main road and on the *platia*. On the village square there is a bust of Odysseus, a board explaining his *Odyssey* home and a model showing what his palace could have looked like 3,250 years ago. A cul-de-sac leads you down to the bay of *Polis*. *D8*

8 KIONI ⭐

Kioni is regarded by many as the most beautiful place on the island. The village lies at the end of a bay surrounded by olive and cypress trees. Here you can rent motor boats and head out to some picturesque bays: on foot or by boat you can reach several small pebble beaches in just a few minutes. In summer, ferries connect the neighbouring village of *Frikes* to Lefkada. *D8*

9 ANOGI ★

The small mountain village lies about 500m high on a plateau strewn with bizarre boulders, some as large as 8m in diameter. Some of these spindle-shaped megaliths show traces from the last ice age. Close by is a church with 17th-century frescoes. *D8*

10 MONASTERY OF KATHARON

The monastery sits at an altitude of 556m and its freestanding bell tower has the most amazing views over large parts of the island. *Mon–Fri 8am–8.30pm | D9*

EATING & DRINKING

LOCALSKOUZINA

The former Gyradiko Kalkanis has been taken over by the young generation. Now they serve not just crisp *gyros* in pita bread and grilled food, but also salads and veggie burgers in a brioche bun. *Vathi | Kallinivou, near the National Bank | €–€€ | D9*

INSIDER TIP
Happy place for vegetarians

MILLS RESTAURANT

Located right on the harbour front, this taverna is a feast for the eyes. Traditional recipes are given a creative twist. *Kioni | harbour front | FB: Mills Restaurant Ithaki | €€ | D8*

SIRINES

Great selection of dishes, very tasty roast pork – *sofrito*, with garlic, mustard and pepper sauce, as is customary on the Ionian Islands. *Vathi | alleyway parallel to the waterfront promenade | sirines.eu | €€€ | D9*

TREHANTIRI

Every morning, home-grown food is freshly cooked and baked in this traditional taverna. Locals like to come here at lunchtime for the cheap vegetable dishes and the cosy atmosphere. *Vathi | alleyway parallel to the coastal road near the post office | €–€€ | D9*

SHOPPING

TEHNIMA

Regarded as the best jeweller on all the islands, this studio, run by Dimosthenis Gkanasoulis, is housed in a 500-year-old stone building. Decorative Greek jewellery and accessories. *Kioni | harbour front | tehnima.com | D8*

SPORT & ACTIVITIES

HIKING

Ester van Zuylen offers guided hikes from different starting points. The Homer Tour is popular and leads you high up into the mountains near *Exogi* village with views of Fiskardo on Kefalonia. *islandwalks.com*

MOTOR BOATS

Motor boats up to 30hp can be hired from *Kioni Boat Hire (Vathi | tel. 69 77 28 08 22 | ithacaboats.com)* without a boating licence.

BEACHES

AGIOS IOANNIS BEACH ✳🐾

A 100m-long, 15m-wide isolated pebble beach northwest of Vathi, unspoilt, without a taverna, but with some good snorkelling when the sea is calm. ▥ *D9*

FILIATRO BEACH 👥

Really nice, child-friendly pebble beach backed by old olive trees and a café, north-east of Vathi. Bear in mind that at the height of summer there are sometimes lots of people and loud music. ▥ *E9*

GIDAKI BEACH ✳🐾

This very beautiful sand-and-pebble beach north-east of Vathi is only accessible on foot or by boat. In midsummer a small beach bar opens. ▥ *E9*

NIGHTLIFE

Theatre performances and concerts are occasionally held in Vathi at the *Morfiko Kentro* (Educational Centre) or the *Kipos Gymnasiou*. The place to go for cocktails is the *Apagkio Café Bar (Anastasiou Kallinivou/corner of Vlachernon | tel. 26 74 03 37 21).*

TRAVEL

FERRY CONNECTIONS

Year-round connections between Pisoaetos and Sami (Kefalonia), Killini/ Peloponnese and Nidri (Lefkada). *Information: harbour police (Vathi | tel. 26 74 03 29 09) or Delas Tours (Vathi | tel. 26 74 03 21 04).*

Exogi in the north of Ithaca has fabulous sea views

LEFKADA

INTERPLAY OF LAND & SEA

Lefkada (pop. 24,000) is the only one of the Ionian Islands that is connected to the mainland. And it is proof of the Greek art of improvisation: instead of building an expensive bridge, they converted an appropriately sized ferry and berthed it sideways in the 50m-wide channel that has made Lefkada an island since Roman times.

Behind the fortress by the channel is a coastal area with miles of dunes stretching towards the north – popular with windsurfers.

The lively tourist resort of Nidri also has a few quiet corners

You can look forward to dreamlike beaches in the west, and sensational sandy coves with chalk cliffs and surfing centres, such as Vassiliki, while Lefkada Town is a hotspot for sailors and sun worshippers with an interest in partying. More action can be found paragliding above the deep blue Ionian Sea. If you are looking for peace and quiet, venture into the wooded mountains and remote villages with ancient stone houses. What are you waiting for?

LEFKADA

Ammoudia   Ammoudia
17   Beach

ΙΟΝΙΟ
ΠΕΛΑΓΟΣ
ΙΟΝΙΟ
PELAGOS

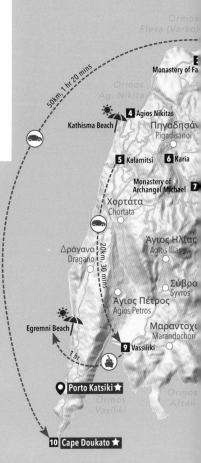

Ormos
Fleva (Varko)

Monastery of Fa

50km, 1 hr 20 mins

Ormos
Ag. Nikita

4 Agios Nikitas

Kathisma Beach

Πηγαδισάν
Pigadisanoi

5 Kalamitsi   6 Karia

Monastery of
Archangel Michael   7

Χορτάτα
Chortata

Άγιος Ηλίας
Agios Ilias

Δράγανο
Dragano

20km, 30 mins

Σύβρο
Syvros

Άγιος Πέτρος
Agios Petros

Μαραντοχ
Marandochori

Egremni Beach

1 hr

9 Vassiliki

Porto Katsiki ★

Ormos
Vassiliki

Ormos
Afteli

10 Cape Doukato ★

5 km
3.11 mi

Relax in the shaded courtyard of the Monastery of Faneromenis

SIGHTSEEING

🔟 LEFKADA TOWN ★

The special charm of the island's capital (pop. 7,000) lies in its position between the lagoon on the north side and the narrow strait that separates Lefkada from the mainland. A balmy easterly wind blows through the cobbled alleyways of the town: the lively pedestrian zone of *Ioannou Mela* is a street lined with two-storey houses painted in pastel shades. For more than 200 years, unlike the rest of the Ionian Islands, Lefkada was part of the Ottoman Empire. Also unlike the other islands, it belonged to Venice only briefly, although a few churches from the Venetian period do remain.

The town's promenade ends at the *platia*, the town's social centre, with kiosks and cafés. To the right of the Naos Agiou Spiridona church, *Odos Dimarchou Verioti* lane begins, with its artisan shops – from icon painters to dental technicians. You can watch people at work through the shop windows.

In the town's maze of alleyways you can also find unusual restaurants such as *Ev Zyn (Filarmonikis 8 | €€)*.

There are plenty of opportunities for shopping: the ☂ market lane *(agora)*, with many clothes shops, runs downhill to the promenade where, on summer evenings, people meet in the numerous cafés and bars at the fishing harbour.

The end of the promenade is marked by the small ☂ *Archaeological Museum (Wed–Sun 8am–3.30pm | admission 3 euros | northern end of the shoreline road | ⏱ 45 mins)*. Here, in the cultural centre building, the most important finds from the island are on display, and many of them come with fascinating information. Colourful walls form the backdrop for terracotta dolls from child tombs from the fifth century BCE and, while antique musical instruments will stir your imagination, sadly they are not accompanied by audio recordings. *D3*

2 AGIA MAVRA

The impressive island fortress of Agia Mavra, dating from the 13th century, used to protect Lefkada Town at the channel between the mainland and the causeway. From its thick walls you can see the queues of cars waiting to enter and leave the island via the ferry-bridge, and boats waiting to pass through when the bridge is raised, as well as the many yachts off the town's harbour promenade with its popular restaurants. Between the end of September and mid-May, flamingos can be spotted standing in the shallow water. *Wed-Mon 8am-7.30pm | admission 3 euros | D-E3*

3 MONASTERY OF FANEROMENIS

The only monastery on the island that is still occupied lies in a small grove above the lagoon and town. It has recently been extensively restored and now includes a beautiful garden and a small, but fine museum. In a small animal park children can get excited about the deer, squirrels and chickens. *4km west of Lefkada Town on the road to Agios Nikitas | closed daily 2–4pm | D3*

4 AGIOS NIKITAS

The only seaside resort (pop. 110) on the west coast by the open sea is nestled in a valley so narrow that there is only enough space for a single (pedestrian) street. The beach in front of the pretty resort is about 50m long; a longer sandy beach stretches to the north. It tends to get crowded and is especially popular with tourists with camper vans. *C4*

5 KALAMITSI

The small inland village (pop. 200) above the long sandy beach of *Kathisma* lies 380m above the west coast. It seems very rural: chickens, goats and donkeys wander freely through the gardens and fields, and the whole village has a rustic vibe. However, it also has a number of guesthouses as well as private rooms for hire. Why not stay for a while to soak up the fabulous views and rural life? **INSIDER TIP The good life** *C4*

6 KARIA

The largest mountain village (pop. 1,000) on the island still has many traditional houses. The village square is shaded by old plane trees, has a good taverna and is full of life in late afternoon. At the top end of the village there is also a small *Folklore Museum (daily 9am–9pm | admission 3 euros | FB: folkloremuseumkaruas | ⏱ 45 mins)*, where the ancient art of weaving is explained in detail: inspiring for anyone interested in arts, crafts and fashion!

After your visit, continue uphill by

Nidri waterfall is a thin trickle in summer

car round hair-raising bends to the limestone mountains of the *Elati* range, whose highest point is 1,158m. Up here, close to *Englouvi* village, locals grow and sell lentils, which are regarded as the best in all of Greece. ▢ D4

INSIDER TIP
Best lentils in Greece

7 MONASTERY OF ARCHANGEL MICHAEL

The island's atmospheric ruins of the Moni Tou Asomatou Archaggelou Mixail (signposted as the "Monastery of the Taxiarches") are situated in a secluded forest setting halfway between Nidri and Englouvi, close to Vafkeri village. Built in the 17th century, the monastery was once home to dozens of monks. High walls and archways are what remain of the monastery. You won't find a nicer picnic spot on the whole of the island. *Signposted on the road from Karia to Vafkeri on a left-hand bend shortly before reaching Vafkeri* | ▢ D5

INSIDER TIP
Ideal picnic spot

8 NIDRI

The liveliest holiday resort on the island (and also its main ferry terminal) is scenically situated opposite several islets at the entrance to the green-fringed bay of *Vlicho*. Its bustling centre is the harbour, where car ferries depart for Meganisi, Ithaca, Kefalonia and other islands, as well as the unbeatable Egremni beach on the west coast, which is currently only accessible by sea. This is also where you can find excursion boats to the island of Skorpios, previously owned by the Onassis family. In the town there is a modern *monument* to Aristotle Onassis (1906–75), the famous Greek shipping magnate, billionaire and husband of Jacqueline Kennedy.

Some 3km away is the *waterfall* (signposted). From the car park you hike for 15 minutes on a well-maintained trail to the rocky place where, in summer, the water runs in a tiny trickle down the mossy rock face. The waterfall is fuller in autumn, spring and winter. If the cool breeze up there isn't cooling enough, you can get refreshments in the shady forest taverna *Platanos* by the car park. *D5*

9 VASSILIKI

In high season, up to 600 windsurfers ride the rough waves every day on the miles-long pebble beach at Vassiliki (pop. 370). The beach

Timing is everything

is at its quietest in the morning – an ideal time for beginners to go out to sea.

Ferries leave for other Ionian Islands and small boats head to the island's dream beaches from the recently modernised port. *C6*

10 CAPE DOUKATO ★

The white chalk cliffs of the *Lefkata Peninsula* offer some of the most beautiful coastal scenery in Greece. The road south to Cape Doukato, past *Athani* village and the island's best beaches at *Porto Katsiki* and *Egremni* (the latter only accessible by boat), is an experience in itself. At Cape Doukato you'll find a car park just a few steps from the bright white lighthouse by the 60m-tall cliffs. Dating from 1890, the lighthouse overlooks the ships that pass by on the route between Italy and the Gulf of Patras. In antiquity this was the site of a temple dedicated to Apollo. According to legend, it was here that Sappho, the first female poet in world literature, committed suicide. The cape is particularly atmospheric at sunset. *C6-7*

EATING & DRINKING

FRINI STO MOLO

Proprietor Frini may be the quickest and snappiest restaurant owner on the island. She displays her creativity in the kitchen with dishes such as a lentil salad with *savoro*, a marinated fish served cold. *Lefkada Town | Odos Golemos 12 (coastal road opposite the pier) | €€ | D3*

LIGHTHOUSE

A small, well-established taverna with a sheltered garden where you can sit quietly and enjoy delicious Greek specialities. Host Sotiris spent some time in Washington DC and speaks excellent English. Booking recommended. *Daily from 5pm | Lefkada Town | Odos Filarmonikis 14 | tel. 26 45 02 51 17 | €€ | D3*

LIOTRIVI

Housed in a former olive mill at Sivota (a settlement in a narrow bay, not to be confused with the village of the same name on the nearby Greek west coast), this café offers the perfect place to spend an afternoon relaxing with sandwiches and cocktails, watching the yachts coming into the port. In the on-site gallery you can visit one of the changing exhibitions and purchase crafts. *Sivota Lefkadas | shoreline road at the south-eastern end | liotrivi. gr | €€ | D6*

OASIS

Forest taverna with tables under the trees. Lamb and goat from the venue's own butchery, and home made cheese. *Athani to Porto Katsiki road, 8km from Athani* | €€ | ⊞ C6

O PLATANOS

This garden tavern, owned by an Athenian dentist and amateur chef, has become an institution. 🐷 You can taste the starters and classic dishes on the terrace, with prices staring at 4 euros. If you are really hungry, you will need to wait for the evening – the grill is fired up from 7pm. *Vafkeri | at the church on the main road | tel. 26 45 04 14 92* | €–€€ | ⊞ D5

RACHI

This venue impresses with its fantastic views of the sea and the coastal hamlet of Kalamitsi from the terrace. The owners make their own wine and olive oil, and vegetables are grown locally. Their produce is also for sale. *Exanthia | entrance to the village | rachi. gr* | €€ | ⊞ C4

SESOULA

Host Georgia serves her guests vegetables and salads from her own garden. Even the chickens are from her coop, and the meat is also local. With simple peasant dishes, such as *pastitsio* (Greek-style lasagne made with beef ragu and macaroni) or stuffed tomatoes and peppers, Sesoula is so authentic that it feels like the Greece of yesteryear. *Dragano | main road* | € | ⊞ C5

SHOPPING

KREOPOLIO POLYCHRONOPOULOS ⚑

Looking for a local delicacy as a souvenir? Lefkada is famous in Greece for its air-dried salami. You can buy it straight from the manufacturer here – for your next picnic or simply to enjoy back home. *Lefkada Town | Odos Mel 180* | ⊞ D3

LEFKADITIKI GI 🐷

This romantic winery, with its old stone buildings and small exhibition, has a mountain setting. On a guided tour you learn how the red Vertzami and white Vardea grapes are produced, and afterwards you can taste the wine they make for free. *4km north of Sivota | lefkaditikigi.gr* | ⊞ D6

INSIDER TIP
Wine and knowledge

On Lefkada Beach, the kitesurfers rule the waves

POTOPIIA FRANGOULI ⚑

This traditional shop, run by the Frangoulis family, is also a distillery. The ouzo, brandy and various liqueurs that you can buy here are produced on site. *Lefkada Town | Odos Mitropleos 4 | ⫿⫿ D3*

QUATTRO LINEA

Vivienne Westwood, the mother of punk fashion, surprisingly showcases her collection at this Lefkada boutique. *Lefkada Town | Odos Mela 114 | FB | ⫿⫿ D3*

STAVRAKAS

The Stavrakas family has been making Lefkadian sweets for more than 60 years. You absolutely have to try the fig salami made with honey and nuts, as well as the sugar-free chocolate with prunes. In the ice-cream parlour next door, they sell the most delicious waffles. *Lefkada Town | Odos Derpfeld 22 | stavrakasweets.gr | ⫿⫿ D3*

SPORT & ACTIVITIES

Lefkada is a mecca for wind- and kite-surfers, especially at Lefkada Town and Vassiliki *(see p. 37)*.

The best place for parasailing, waterskiing and wakeboarding is the *Dennis Watersports Centre (FB)* in Nidri. Tandem paragliding is on offer at Rachi restaurant *(see p. 94)* or on Kathisma Beach *(flyfeel.gr)*.

Boat tours are a very popular activity: from Nidri there are *trips (Borsalino Travel Nidri | borsalinotravel.gr)* to ⟡ *Egremni Beach* on the west coast which, since the 2015 earthquake, has only been accessible from the sea.

The Meganisi ferry takes you to the first-ever private island in Greece: *Skorpios (see p. 97).* A 🐷 return trip is

Meganisi: so pretty that you'd better visit before they start charging admission!

only around 7 euros, and you will get to see Meganisi as well.

BEACHES

The island's most beautiful beaches are on the south-western peninsula at *Porto Katsiki*, *Gialos* and ⭐ *Egremni Beach*, which is currently only accessible by boat. Near the ferry-bridge joining the island to the mainland, you can bathe on Lefkada spit north of the lagoon. Swimming is also possible at the surfers' bay of *Vassiliki*.

Other popular beaches include *Agios Nikitas*, ⭐ *Kathisma Beach* and *Poros Beach*, 5km below the village of the same name on the south coast. Less frequented is the pebble beach at *Milos*, which one can reach on foot from Agios Nikitas (25-minute walk).

Between Athani and Cape Doukato,

a road turns off to the cove of ⭐ *Porto Katsiki*, a light-coloured band of sand deep below the white chalk cliffs. Its image is frequently used to advertise Greece as an international tourist destination.

NIGHTLIFE

Lefkada has a number of great venues for a night out on the town. In Lefkada Town, you can go clubbing at *Karma (Odos Derpfeld 1)*, with international mainstream music, while at the *Taratsa Open Bar (shoreline promenade | roof terrace of Café Margarita)* they play funk. On the shoreline north of the Archaeological Museum, the *Capital Club (Odos Ang. Sikelianou 4)*, with a pool, open-air bar and spacious dancefloors, awaits; it also features Greek pop stars. In the old town's maze of alleyways, people dance salsa on summer evenings at the *Cubana Salsa Bar (Odos Verioti 6/ Pinelopis 4)*. They offer 12 different mojitos and 10 varieties of rum, plus a selection of cigars. The venue includes the *Mavros Lagos* wine bar, with a large list of Greek wines. In Nidri, the open-air bar and café *Sail-Inn (beach, direction Lefkada Town | sailinn.com.gr)* is a lively day-time meeting place which plays dance music from 9pm. A cosier atmosphere can be found at the *Roadhouse music bar (southern end of the main through road)*.

PIRATES

This cool and rocking boat bar on two decks of a replica sailing ship is open day and night. Music is played in the evening, and on Thursdays they lay on a house lounge. There is a second venue in *Sivota* cove. *Lefkada Town shoreline | FB: Pirates Lefkada | ᗕ D3*

AROUND LEFKADA

⓫ SKORPIOS

1 hr by boat from Nidri (Lefkada)

By the summer of 2024 the former private island of the Onassis family – now owned by Russian oligarch Dmitry Rybolovlev – should have been converted into a VIP luxury resort with villas, conference centres, an amphitheatre and a helipad, at a cost of 165m euros. A glance at the private beaches and roofs of the buildings from a boat stirs the imagination in terms of how, once upon a time, one of the wealthiest men on earth, Greek-Argentine shipping magnate Aristotle Onassis, lived here – initially with opera diva Maria Callas and later with Jackie Onassis, widow of John F Kennedy. Excursion boats are even permitted to briefly dock at one of the island's beaches. You can take a boat trip from Nidri *(1hr | from 40 euros | odysseialefkada.eu)*, or a day trip from Nidri to Kastos and Kalamos via Formikoula, Skorpios, Sparti and Madouri *(7–8 hrs | from 25 euros | borsalinotravel.gr)*. A single ferry journey from Nidri to Meganisi goes past Skorpios *(4 times daily | single ticket 2 euros | borsalinotravel.gr)*. ᗕ E5

⓬ MEGANISI ★

Approx. 1 hr/10km by car and ferry from Nidri (Lefkada) to Spartochori

Meganisi (pop. 500) is the largest of the islets between Lefkada and the mainland. The billionaire Lord Jacob Rothschild has bought 500 hectares in the island's south, where he hopes to entice other billionaires to build unique, exclusive villas. However, for now, the island is open to everyone. Most ferries stop at *Porto Spilia* harbour. A 20-minute walk leads to the pretty inland village of *Spartochori*, and a further 60-minute walk will take you to the second village, *Katomeri*. ᗕ E5–6

13 KALAMOS

30 mins by ferry from Mitikas (mainland)

The mini island of Kalamos has only 580 permanent residents. However, in summer it can get busy as many local people come to stay in their holiday homes with magnificent views – the highest point on Kalamos is at 785m. The island's hills are covered in pine forest and there are almost no cars. In the south, the pebble beach of *Agrapida*, framed by ancient windmills and olive trees, invites you to take a dip. Further north is a second settlement: the hamlet of *Episkopi* with its small pebble beaches. The road there leads through verdant hillside vegetation and the area is ideal for hiking. There

INSIDER TIP
Immersed in the greenery

are connections to Kalamos from Mitikas (mainland), and in the summer some trips are organised from Lefkada, for example, an island-hopping day trip from Nidri that includes Kastos (greeka.com). Sea taxis from Mitikas harbour can be hired from Georgios Giannoutsos (*single 50 euros | tel. 69 77 84 59 46*). ⥂ *F–G6*

14 KASTOS

50 mins by ferry from Mitikas (mainland)

The smallest isle in the Ionian Islands is almost car-free. There are a few tavernas and bars for the sailors who like to dock in the west in the natural cove of *Sarakiniko*, with its small pier, in search of heavenly peace. Entertainment, catering and accommodation are available in private holiday homes and rented rooms. The best location to stay is the island's largest settlement, *Kastos*, near the small sand and pebble beaches that are accessible on foot. *Regular ferry connections (3 euros | chanialines.com) from Mitikas (mainland) via Kalamos. Occasional boat excursions from Lefkada in summer (greeka.com).* ⥂ *F6–7*

15 PREVEZA

27km from Lefkada Town/35 mins by car or 60 mins by bus

Preveza (pop. 15,000) is a small mainland town surrounded by the sea on three sides. It is located at the mouth of the Ambracian Gulf, a body of water which stretches over 35km inland. An undersea tunnel under the mouth of the gulf connects the town to the mainland on other side. Here, a small fort marks the site of ancient *Actium*, which gave the sea battle – and now also the airport – its name.

A stroll through the main shopping street to the small market hall and nice lanes with alternative cafés is worthwhile. Many of the houses date back to the 19th century; in the *Agios Athanassios* church there are some murals. The 🎯 *Luna Park (daily from 6pm | Spiliadou 2 | ⏱ 30–60 mins)*, with bumper cars and a Ferris wheel, is great fun for all. *Buses from Lefkada Town to Preveza run several times daily | ⥂ E2*

16 NIKOPOLIS ⭐

36km from Lefkada Town/45 mins by car or 60 mins by bus

These impressive remains from

antiquity are just 9km from Preveza on the mainland. The site is easily reached by bus from *Lefkada Town*. The trip is worthwhile even for those who are not particularly interested in archaeology.

Nikopolis was founded in 30 BCE by Octavian, the future Roman Emperor Augustus, to commemorate his naval victory over Antony and Cleopatra, and it was settled until the 13th century. The city enjoyed its heyday during the early Byzantine period in the years between CE 500 and 600. Some of the foundation walls, stone carvings and mosaic floors of the basilicas dating from that era have been preserved. However, the most impressive of the remains are the Byzantine city wall, with its well-preserved gates and towers. The amphitheatre (not currently accessible but visible from the outside due to its hillside location) is also testimony to the size of the city. *City excavations daily 8am–7pm, city walls freely accessible | Preveza–Arta road, 9km from Preveza | admission 8 euros, combined ticket with the excavation museum | odysseus.culture.gr | ⏱ 2–3 hrs | 🗺 D–E1*

🔢 AMMOUDIA

70km from Lefkada Town/1 hr by car
The small village (pop. 350) on the mainland coast belongs to the Preveza prefecture. In 2021, its partly) managed, light-coloured 🏖 *Ammoudia Beach* was awarded a Blue Flag. Here, the River Acheron joins the turquoise-and-blue Ionian Sea. According to Greek mythology, the Acheron was one of the five rivers of the underworld. A soul is supposed to sail it in order to be cleansed before its rebirth. Today you can traverse the beautiful and unspoilt nature reserve, which is rich in wildlife, on an Acheron Delta kayak or canoe tour *(1km inland direction Mesapotamos, ancient Nekromanteion | acheronkayak.gr | adults 20 euros, children aged 6–12 10 euros, under-6s free).*

From Ammoudia you can go on other excursions, such as horse riding *(Horse Riding Alonaki | Valanidorrachi | daily by appointment | reiturlaub-griechenland.com | 20 euros/hr)* or wine and oil tasting *(Paragaea | Parga | daily 10am–2pm | paragaea.gr | tour 5 euros, wine tasting 26 euros). 🗺 0*

Kastos promises the ultimate island vibes

DISCOVERY TOURS

Do you want to get under the skin of the islands? Then our discovery tours provide the perfect guide. They include advice on which sights to visit, tips on where to stop for that perfect holiday snap, a choice of the best places to eat and drink, and suggestions for fun activities.

❶ FOUR IONIAN ISLANDS AT A GLANCE

➤ Experience fabulous city flair & a boat trip
➤ Bicycle tour & premium clubbing
➤ Visit a cave with stalactites & hike with donkeys

📍 Zakynthos Town

🏁 Vafkeri

➡ 638km (492km by car/taxi/bus, 125km by bicycle, 21km on foot)

🚗 11 days (24 hrs total driving time)

ℹ Bus timetable Zakynthos: *ktel-zakynthos.gr*; flight Zakynthos–Kefalonia: *skyexpress.gr*; bus timetable Kefalonia: *ktelkefalonias.gr*; ferry Kefalonia–Ithaca: *ionionpelagos.com*; hire car booking Ithaca: *agscars.com*; ferry Ithaca–Lefkada: *borsalinotravel.gr*

Once a smuggling hotspot: Shipwreck Beach on Zakynthos

ARRIVAL AND GETTING IN THE MOOD

Take a taxi from the island's airport to ❶ Zakynthos Town ➤ p.44 *and the* Strada Marina *hotel (strada marina.gr).* To stretch your legs after the flight, *walk up to the panoramic village of* ❷ Bochali ➤ p.45, *which will take you around* 30 minutes, *and enjoy the fabulous views. In the evening, head to the* ⚑ Varkarola ➤ p.61 taverna, where traditional *kantades* are sung to get you in the mood for the trip ahead.

FEASTING, SWIMMING, MINI GOLF

If you are up bright and early and manage to visit the ⚑ Zakynthos Museum ➤ p.45 before 10am, you will be treated to the splendid sight of the museum's icons lit up by the morning sun. After your museum visit, *wander from St Mark's Square and along the main shopping street, Alexandrou Roma,* where you can buy authentic Greek food at ⚑ Ellinon Gefsis ➤ p.55 for a picnic later on. Your next stop is the church of Agios Dionysios ➤ p.44 situated virtually on the harbour front, from where you can *head back along the promenade to your* hotel. Deposit your purchases in your room and enjoy your picnic on the balcony with views of the Peloponnese mountains in the background.

DAY 1
❶ Zakynthos Town
2km 40 mins
❷ Bochali

DAY 2

9km	55 mins
❸ Argassi	

Around 3pm, you can take your first dip in the Ionian Sea *followed by a bus ride to* ❸ Argassi ➤ p. 51. The most romantic spot for a swim is at the old English bridge in front of the Xenos Kamara Beach hotel, where you can enjoy a coffee afterwards on the hotel's poolside terrace. The next activity is mini golf at what is probably one of Europe's craziest mini golf courses ➤ p. 56 (500m from the hotel). Then *return to the* Strada Marina hotel *by bus or taxi*. In the evening, dine at Alesta ➤ p. 53 on St Mark's Square, which serves the best pizzas and salads on the island.

TODAY IT GETS AMPHIBIOUS

Set off in your hire car at 9am at the latest and *head to the island's most northerly point at the lighthouse at* Cape Skinari ➤ p. 47. From here you can take a small motor boat (it has to be small to enter the caves!) to the ❹ Blue Caves ➤ p.47 and even bathe in the magical light inside. Twenty minutes later, swap to a larger speedboat that jets you off to the world-famous ❺ Shipwreck Beach ➤ p.47 where you can spend 45 minutes, including a swim. You'll be back at your car at around 1.30pm and will be ready for a bite to eat at ❻ Taverna Faros *(€€), a two-minute drive from Cape Skinari. Then take the road to Volimes and, on leaving the town, steer towards the coast.* Be brave and enjoy the splendid view from the ❼ Skywalk ("Shipwreck viewpoint") to Shipwreck Beach below. The stalls in front of the skywalk sell Corinthian currants, a perfect snack for the days ahead. *Now drive across the island to reach the taverna* ☂ Fioro tou Levante ➤ p. 53 for an early evening meal. The taverna is on the hill with the church ❽ Ano Gerakari, and its terrace offers splendid views not only of Zakynthos, but of Kefalonia too. A special spot for a nightcap is on one of the balconies of the Bliss Art Café Bar ➤ p.60 in Zakynthos Town.

OFF TO KEFALONIA

Around lunchtime the next day, a propeller plane will fly you at a low height in 10 minutes from Zakynthos to Kefalonia. *Then take a taxi to* ❾ Argostoli ➤ p.66 to spend three nights at the Ionian Plaza *(ionian plaza.com)*, a hotel whose balconies overlook the expansive main square below. Once you have picked up your pre-booked bikes from Aionos Bicycle Store ➤ p.34, *cycle along the bay* to the two seawater mills. One of the two mills houses the chic Katavothres lounge bar ➤ p.67 with international music and tasty cocktails, including non-alcoholic mixes. At sunset, *cycle back into town* and take a seat at one of the tables on the wooden planks outside Kiani Akti ➤ p. 73 and enjoy a meal directly over the water. The seafood is a favourite here.

DAY 3	
43.5km	1 hr
❹ Blue Caves	
12.5km	1 hr 40 mins
❺ Shipwreck Beach	
13km	44 mins
❻ Taverna Faros	
14.5km	25 mins
❼ Skywalk	
26km	40 mins
❽ Ano Gerakari	

DAY 4	
79.5km	1 hr 35 mins
❾ Argostoli	
15km	1 hr 10 mins

VISITING DREAM BEACHES BY BICYCLE

At 9.30am the next day, push your bike onto the ferry and soak in the views on the *20-minute crossing to* ⑩ *Lixouri* ➤ p.72. *Follow the bike signs* to the unique ⑪ Xi Beach ➤ p.77 with its red sand surrounded by light grey cliffs. At the Baywatch Beach House you can hire a canoe or other equipment from Baywatch Watersports ➤ p.77 and spend the next hour gliding through the waters. Then *continue by bike to* ⑫ Vatsa Beach ➤ p.77 with its laid-back hippie atmosphere. First go for a swim and then dine at the beach's only taverna followed by a siesta on the beach. *You'll need 70 to 90 minutes to return to the ferry.* As a treat after all your physical exertions, go for a meal at Paparazzi *(paparazzi-kefalonia.com | €€)* and then music at the Cajablanca Club ➤ p.77

DISCOVER CAVES AND HIKE WITH DONKEYS

Your day starts at 10am and you'll need a hire car to *drive across the island.* The first item on your itinerary is a descent into the ⑬ ⛱ Drogarati Cave ➤ p.70, and then through the ⑭ Melissani Cave ➤ p.71 by boat. Back in daylight, enjoy a meal followed by a refreshing *freddo* espresso lying in a hammock at the sea-front taverna ⑮ Karavomilos ➤ p.71. The next stop is in Grizata around 4pm, where Katharina from ⑯ Donkey Trekking ➤ p.75 will meet you to escort you on a two-hour 🐴 donkey trek. Your final meal on the island can be enjoyed at the elegant Casa Grec restaurant *(€€).*

... AND ON TO ITHACA

Stop in Argostoli for a spot of shopping in the morning and treat yourself to at least one slice of cake from the confectionery shop on the main square. A *public bus running at 1pm will take you to* Sami ➤ p.70, from where a ferry departs around 2.45pm to Pisaetos on Ithaca. You should find your pre-booked hire car waiting for you at the port. *Drive to the* Hotel Mentor *(hotelmentor.gr)* in the island town of ⑰ Vathi ➤ p.82 where you will spend two nights (remember to book in advance). For a swim in the late afternoon, *drive along the south side of the port bay*

DAY 5	
⑩ Lixouri	
8km	35 mins
⑪ Xi Beach	
7km	30 mins
⑫ Vatsa Beach	

DAY 6	
40km	1 hr 30 mins
⑬ Drogarati-Caves	
6km	10 mins
⑭ Melissani Caves	
500m	1 min
⑮ Karavomilos	
6.5 km	10 mins
⑯ Donkey Trekking	
69.5km	2 hrs 5 mins

DAY 7	
⑰ Vathi	
2.5km	5 mins

Zen, Greek style: try a donkey instead of yoga

and follow the sign to  **Loutsa Beach**. The 20-m pebble beach is just wide enough for a plunge. Stop *on your way back* at the taverna **Localskouzina** ➤ p. 84 for an authentic Greek meal with hearty dishes.

⑱ Loutsa Beach	
16km	20 mins

BE YOUR OWN CAPTAIN

Today you can explore Odysseus's island of birth *by hire car*. After a brief visit inside the **⑲ Katharon Monastery** ➤ p. 84 and the church **⑳ Anogi** ➤ p. 84, head to **㉑ Kioni** ➤ p. 83, the island's prettiest fishing village. Following lunch at **Mills** ➤ p. 84, it's worth browsing around **Tehnima** ➤ p. 84, ranked as one of the best jewellers in Greece, before hiring a motor boat and playing at being your own captain. You have three hours to explore the region's tiny beaches and coves at your leisure. *Now drive back to Vathi along the island's west coast* and dine in the evening at the **Sirines taverna** ➤ p. 84, before you soak in the views over the idyllic bay in the moonlight from your balcony.

DAY 8	
⑲ Katharon Monastery	
3.5km	5 mins
⑳ Anogi	
13km	15 mins
㉑ Kioni	

ACTIVE AND RELAXED IN NIDRI

At 9am today, *a taxi takes you to* **Frikes** in the island's north. *From there, take a ferry at 10.15am to*

DAY 9	
74.5km	2 hrs 55 mins

㉒ Nidri	**㉒ Nidri** ➤ p. 92 *on Lefkada*. The crossing takes around two hours. Your hotel for the next three nights is the Nydrion Beach *(nydrionbeach.gr), located just 5 minutes on foot from the ferry terminal*. The hotel stands on the seafront, the perfect location for a quick swim before lunch at the portside restaurant Piperi *(€€)*. Sport is on this afternoon's agenda. Dennis Watersports Centre ➤ p. 95 at the northern end of the village offers parasailing sessions for the more adventurous visitors. Two-seater kites are also available for hire. After your thrilling experience, you can relax next door in the Sail-Inn ➤ p. 97 beach club before returning to the port for your evening meal.
11km 1 hr 35 mins	

GET SOME SUN AND HAVE AN ADVENTURE

<table>
<tr><td>DAY 10</td><td rowspan="6">Treat yourself to a relaxing day by the sea today. The excursion boat from Borsalino Travel ➤ p. 95 departs at 9.30am and ferries you to the island of ㉓ Meganisi ➤ p. 97 and to the beaches on the privately owned island of ㉔ Skorpios ➤ p. 97, which once belonged to Aristotle Onassis and now to a Russian business magnate. The crew prepares a filling BBQ on board for guests. You return to Nidri around 5.30pm, from where you can take the bus in the evening to the island's capital ㉕ Lefkada Town ➤ p. 90. Start your evening chilling out in Caribbean style at the Cubana Salsa Bar ➤ p. 97, followed by an evening meal at the taverna Lighthouse ➤ p. 93. If you want to party, head to the Pirates ➤ p. 97 club boat. You will need to take a taxi to return to Nidri.</td></tr>
<tr><td>㉓ Meganisi</td></tr>
<tr><td>4km   15 mins</td></tr>
<tr><td>㉔ Skorpios</td></tr>
<tr><td>19km   25 mins</td></tr>
<tr><td>㉕ Lefkada Town</td></tr>
</table>

FROM A DREAM BEACH TO AN ANCIENT MOUNTAIN VILLAGE

<table>
<tr><td>DAY 11</td><td rowspan="6">Start your day at 9am with a tour of the island by hire car. Drive past the island's capital and up to ㉖ Faneromenis Monastery ➤ p. 91 with its small animal park and fantastic panoramic views. Then drive down to Agios Nikitas and then up along the west coast to the lighthouse at the most south-westerly point of ㉗ Cape Doukato ➤ p. 93. The photogenic ㉘ Porto Katsiki beach ➤ p. 96 below the steep coastline is the perfect spot for a swim. Head back on the main road to</td></tr>
<tr><td>36km   50 mins</td></tr>
<tr><td>㉖ Faneromenis Monastery</td></tr>
<tr><td>44.5km   45 mins</td></tr>
<tr><td>㉗ Cape Doukato</td></tr>
<tr><td>9.5km   25 mins</td></tr>
<tr><td>㉘ Porto Katsiki Beach</td></tr>
</table>

eat and relax in splendid surroundings at the forest taverna Oasis ➤ p. 93. Liotrivi ➤ p. 93 above ㉙ Sivota bay is a pleasant café to enjoy a coffee and watch the yachts sailing in and out of the bay. *Return to Nidri, and drive to the waterfalls for a quick dip in the fresh water – a change after all the sea water. A narrow road leads uphill to the mountain village of* ㉚ Vafkeri, where you can spend your final evening on this trip at the authentically Greek village taverna O Platanos ➤ p. 94. Be daring and order *frigadeli*, pieces of liver in intestines – a hearty island speciality.

24km	30 mins
㉙ Sivota	
28km	1 hr 5 mins
㉚ Vafkeri	

❷ A DAY WITH THE TURTLES ON ZAKYNTHOS

➤ Explore the Marine National Park
➤ Encounter turtles while kayaking
➤ Romantic dinner or party?

| 📍 Zakynthos Town | 🏁 Kalamaki Beach |
| → 80km | 🚗 13 hrs (2½ hrs total driving time) |

ℹ️ What to pack: swimwear.
Kayak hire: *tel. 26 95 02 66 26 | villa-nostos.com*
Alternative to kayaking: guided boat tour from Laganas Beach, departs every half hour, 25 euros.
The tour can also be done by motorbike or scooter.

GET USEFUL INFORMATION

From ❶ Zakynthos Town ➤ p. 44 *drive via Argassi to the Skopos Peninsula, where the narrow and bendy road ends at* ❷ Gerakas Beach ➤ p. 58. The small private exhibition at the Mediterranean Marine Life Centre informs visitors about the sea turtles and land turtles and about the flora and fauna on the land areas of the Marine National Park. The staff of the national park welcome visitors to the beach, explain how they

❶ Zakynthos Town	
16km	15 mins
❷ Gerakas Beach	
4km	15 mins

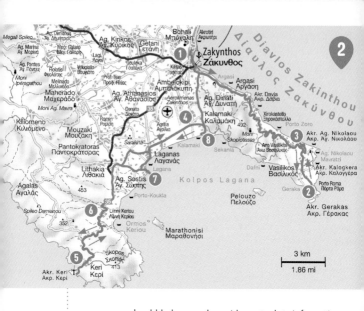

should behave and provide up-to-date information on, for example, the current number of turtle nests on the beach. For an early lunchtime snack, *drive back towards town* and stop for a break at the well-signposted ❸ Banána Beach Bar ➤ p. 57.

❸ Banana Beach Bar

PADDLE WITH TURTLES

16km 20 mins
❹ Kalamaki

Continue past Argassi to the Bay of ❹ Kalamaki ➤ p. 51. Book a kayak in advance from Eco Zante *(tel. 26 95 10 05 03 | ecozante.com)* and go to the agreed meeting point on the beach where your hire kayak will be ready for you. Paddle along the beach close to the harbour for the next hour. Between July and September, you have a good chance of seeing loggerhead turtles (*Caretta caretta*, p. 53) swimming in the water below. But don't worry: you will not disturb the creatures with your paddling. After your kayak tour, *cross Laganas* and drive to the lighthouse at

INSIDER TIP
Meet the turtles

19.5km 35 mins
❺ Keri

❺ Keri ➤ p. 52. Take a seat at the *cantina* on one of the straw bales and enjoy the panoramic views along the coastline. On your way back, stop at the taverna To Fanari tou Keriou *(€€)*, where you will see the Greek flag flying on calmer days. A short skywalk over a glass floor offers the perfect location for fantastic photos of the cliffs at Mizithres – provided you are brave enough.

TAR SPRINGS, COCKTAILS AND ROMANCE
Make make sure to briefly visit the 🐵 🐟 Pechquelle in ❻ Limni Keriou ➤ p. 53 – it's said to bring good luck. *Then head to the port of Laganas, Porto Sostis. An adventurous bridge takes you on foot* to the privately owned island that's home to the ❼ Cameo Clubs *(€)*, where you can relax to the sounds of house music. The taverna Zakanthi *(€–€€)* on the main road to Kalamaki near ❽ Kalamaki Beach welcomes guests to its romantic garden in the evening. With a little luck (which you have hopefully taken with you from the tar spring), a DJ will entertain you afterwards at the 111 cocktail bar ➤ p. 59.

8km	10 mins
❻ **Limni Keriou**	
9km	15 mins
❼ **Cameo Clubs**	
7.5km	30 mins
❽ **Kalamaki Beach**	

❸ ITHACA – IN THE FOOTSTEPS OF ODYSSEUS

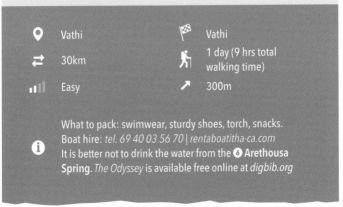

➤ Boat trip in the footsteps of Odysseus
➤ Hike in unspoilt nature
➤ Evening relaxation

📍 Vathi

🏁 Vathi

⇄ 30km

🚶 1 day (9 hrs total walking time)

▮▮▮ Easy

↗ 300m

ℹ️ What to pack: swimwear, sturdy shoes, torch, snacks.
Boat hire: tel. 69 40 03 56 70 | rentaboatitha-ca.com
It is better not to drink the water from the ❹ Arethousa Spring. *The Odyssey* is available free online at *digbib.org*

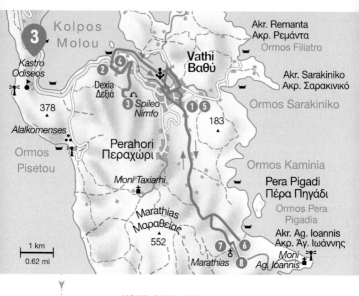

YOUR OWN LITTLE ADVENTURE

Like elsewhere in Greece, you do not need a licence or previous experience to hire a motor boat on the island. From ❶ Vathi ➤ p.82, *cruise to* ❷ Dexia Beach ➤ p.82, where Odysseus first set foot on the island laden with treasure after his epic ten-year journey. Luckily, your baggage is somewhat lighter for the *50-minute hike up to the* ❸ Grotto of the Nymphs ➤ p.82, where Odysseus once hid his treasures. After this demanding walk, enjoy a refreshing swim at ❹ Dexia Beach, before you spend a little time cruising around the Bay of Vathi.

TRACING ANCIENT LEGENDS

Once you have returned the motor boat, it's time for a bite to eat in ❺ Vathi at the market taverna Trehantiri ➤ p.84, where food is freshly cooked every day. Your second hike of the day now starts at the promenade where you will see a signpost reading *"9 Anemodouri–Arethousa Krini"* shortly before the Hotel Mentor. *Follow this sign out of town along the well-paved road, where you will see another sign to the* ❻ Arethousa Spring ➤ p.82. You'll need to follow

Sidebar itinerary:

❶ Vathi
  3km · 20 mins
❷ Dexia Beach
  3km · 1 hr 25 mins
❸ Grotto of the Nymphs
  3km · 1 hr
❹ Dexia Beach
  3.5km · 25 mins
❺ Vathi
  7km · 2 hrs 10 mins
❻ Arethousa Spring

the narrow, stony path for a good two hours to reach the spring. This is where – according to legend – Eumaeus, Odysseus's swineherd, grazed his master's pigs. *When you return to the road, follow it for around 900m to the left* until you reach the rugged ❼ Marathias plateau, with a gun emplacement from World War II. A broken signpost indicates the short path to ❽ Eumaeus Cave, where the faithful herdsman supposedly once lived.

3km	1 hr 15 mins
❼ **Marathias**	
200m	10 mins
❽ **Eumaeus Cave**	
7km	2 hrs
❶ **Vathi**	

LOVELY VIEWS
To return, you need to *backtrack for around 90 minutes* to ❶ Vathi ➤ p. 82 and your room with sea view at the Hotel Mentor *(hotelmentor.gr)*. You can stock up at the supermarket next door to the hotel on cheese, olives, fruit and tomatoes to enjoy the rest of your evening on your balcony, accompanied by a bottle of wine (and maybe a copy of *The Odyssey*…).

❹ KEFALONIA'S BEAUTIFUL NORTH

➤ Sea views from steep cliffs
➤ Stroll through elegant yachting villages
➤ Bathing break on a dream beach

📍 Argostoli	🏁 Argostoli
⇄ 138km	🚗 1 day (4 hrs total driving time)
ℹ What to pack: swimwear, bathing shoes if needed. The tour can also be done by motorbike.	

HIKING, SWIMMING AND HAVING FUN
The route along the hillsides from ❶ Argostoli ➤ p. 66 *to Assos and Fiskardo is well signposted and steep, uphill and downhill, past the plateau of Kalo Oros to chic* ❷ Assos ➤ p. 71, with its French Riviera feel. Leave your car in the car park and *follow the 40-minute trail up to the* Venetian castle. Afterwards, take a dip from

❶ **Argostoli**	
51.5km	45 mins
❷ **Assos**	
19km	1 hr 10 mins

the village's tiny beach before enjoying a bite to eat at the Platanos taverna ➤ p.72 on the village square, where specialities include *kreatopita* and different island cheeses.

CIRCULAR TRAIL IN FISKARDO

Now *continue through the mountains to* ❸ *Fiskardo* ➤ *p.72 in the far north. Follow the sign to the ferry and park at the end of the road behind the Nicolas taverna. A signposted circular trail* takes you to the small lighthouse and to the ruins of a Gothic church. You'll be back at your car after around 40 minutes and will have time to stroll along the resort's promenade, drink a coffee and see the yachts.

SHOP FOR HERBS AND TAKE SELFIES

Continue inland through Mesovounia up to the mountain village of ❹ Karia. Rosie's Kitchen Bar ➤ p.73 will welcome you with a freshly made thyme or lemon balm herbal tea. There is no better place to purchase the island's herbs to take home as a souvenir. After this revitalising brew, *take the road along the east coast towards Agia Efimia to Xiropotamos and then follow the signs to Divarata. From here, a winding road leads you down the cliffs to* ❺ Mirtos Beach ➤ p.77 – one of the most popular and most photographed beaches in Greece. At the start of the winding road is a viewing and selfie point in a layby.

INSIDER TIP
Selfie stop

Drive back to ❶ Argostoli ➤ p.66 an hour before sunset to enjoy the last light of day – driving by night is no fun on Kefalonia due to the poor state of the roads. Once back in town, head to the traditional *mezedopolio* 🚩 🍷 Beverinos ➤ p.73 for a bite to eat.

⑤ LEFKADA – NESTLED BETWEEN BEACH AND MOUNTAINS

➤ **Discover lively mountain villages**
➤ **Enjoy sea views from the mountains**
➤ **Fun water sports & exciting horse trekking**

📍 Lefkada Town	🏁 Milos Beach Club
→ 53km	🚗 12 hrs (3 hrs total driving time)

ℹ What to pack: swimwear, jeans for horse trekking. Book your horse trekking at **⑥ Aramis Farm** (also suitable for beginners) the evening before at the latest: *tel. 69 38 81 61 64.*
The tour can also be done by motorbike.

EXPERIENCE ANCIENT TRADITIONS

From the southern end of the island's biggest town ① Lefkada Town ➤ p. 90, *a road ascends* to the largest of the island's mountain villages, ② Karia ➤ p. 91. In the Folklore Museum you can learn how, in days gone by, the women used to feed their families: by weaving. There even used to be a weaving college here. The old timber-frame house on the edge of the village displays various designs and patterns for traditional costumes, wedding dresses and carpets – some of their "ethnic" styles are popular today. Afterwards, take a seat on the large, shady village square underneath the old plane trees and watch village life pass you by. Some locals still collect water from the pretty village well. The village souvenir shops also sell local woven products that make good presents, and you should definitely buy some fruit and cheese from the general store located directly above the square for your picnic later on in the day. *Continue your drive to* Vafkeri and, *on a left-hand bend just before reaching the village*, you will pass an old ③ well under a big plane tree. It also has a traditional place to do washing and a large basin where

① Lefkada Town
12.5km 15 mins

② Karia

7.5km 30 mins
③ Well

grapes were once crushed underfoot. The next item on your agenda is a stroll through the forest: *follow a small brown signpost along a narrow paved road to* the ruins of the Venetian ❹ **Monastery of the Archangel Michael ➤ p. 92.** Here you can enjoy your picnic in the silent surroundings and lie back on the grass to watch the skies. It's no wonder that the monks who once lived here felt extremely close to the heavens above.

2km	40 mins

❹ Monastery of the Archangel Michael

CROSSING THE SEA ON A SOFA

Now drive through the village of Vafkeri down to ➎ Nidri ➤ p. 92. The views of the sea and the multitude of tiny bays, hundreds of yachts, tiny privately owned islands and the high mainland mountains are simply breathtaking. Then it's time to ride the "crazy sofa" *(20 euros)*, pulled at hair-raising speeds over the water by a motor boat and organised by the Dennis Watersports Centre ➤ p. 95 – there is no time for a nap on this sofa! Now swap your sofa for a saddle and head to ➏ Aramis Farm in Apolpena on the outskirts of Lefkada. If you book in advance, Swedish owner Janet Nikolesi-Berglund will have everything well prepared for you to enjoy a two-hour trek on horseback *(20 euros/ hr)*.

10km 40 mins
➎ **Nidri**
18 km
➏ **Aramis Farm**
3km 20 mins

ATMOSPHERIC FINALE

Time for the evening meal at the ➐ Milos Beach Club *(milosbeach.gr | €)* on the spit of land to the north of the town. Its bar and taverna are the main meeting places for keen windsurfers and kitesurfers, and parties are often held here. If things heat up, the sea is just a stone's throw away to cool down.

➐ **Milos Beach Club**

Nidri offers fabulous sea views

GOOD TO KNOW

HOLIDAY BASICS

ARRIVAL

During the summer there are several regular flights to Zakynthos *(zth-airport.gr)* from the UK. Only a few low-cost and chartered flights go to Aktion (previously Preveza) airport, on the mainland near Lefkada *(pvk-airport.gr)*, and to Kefalonia *(efl-airport. gr)*. There are also some seasonal flights to Araxos airport at Patra/Peloponnese. There are regular flights to Zakynthos, Kefalonia and Lefkada all year round from Athens.

Taxis are available at all airports, but they can also be pre-booked *(lefkas airporttransfers.com)*. Airport buses are available from Aktion *(ktelprevezas.gr)*, as well as from Lefkada to Aktion airport *(ktel-lefkadas.gr)*, and on Kefalonia *(ktelkefalonias.gr)*. You can only get to Ithaca by boat; the best way is from Killini/Peloponnese or Kefalonia.

 + 2 hours ahead

Greece is two hours ahead of Greenwich Mean Time, seven hours ahead of US Eastern Time and seven hours behind Australian Eastern Time.

 Socket type C and F

Greece uses the same socket types as most of Europe. You'll need an adaptor if you're coming from the UK or USA.

Car ferries connect Igoumenitsa on the mainland (for Lefkada) and Patras on the Peloponnese (for the remaining islands) throughout the year with

Blue hour in Zakynthos Town

the Italian ports of Ancona, Brindisi and Bari. A car ferry also departs from Bari for Sami (Kefalonia) several times in July and August. *Ventouris Ferries (tel. 21 04 82 80 01 | ventouris ferries.com)*.

For entry with your own car, a national licence and the motor vehicle registration should suffice; an international green insurance card is recommended. There is a good network of petrol stations on the islands. The use of seatbelts is compulsory. The maximum speed in the towns is 50kmh (30mph), on other roads 90kmh (56mph). The maximum blood alcohol limit is 0.5 for car drivers and 0.1 for motorcycle riders. Parking in a no parking zone is expensive!

CLIMATE & WHEN TO GO

The Ionian Islands are really only suitable as a tourist destination in the late spring and summer months. Since almost all of them depend heavily on tourism, many shops, restaurants and hotels that are not in the island capitals are closed from mid-October until April. During this time the islands can seem eerily empty, transport links are limited and the weather can also be unpleasant due to storms and rainfall.

ENTERING THE COUNTRY

UK, US, Canadian, Australian and New Zealand citizens can enter Greece with a passport – no visa is needed. EU citizens whose country of origin is a member of the Schengen Agreement can use national ID to enter Greece. For up-to-date immigration regulations visit *travel.gov.gr*

TOURIST INFORMATION

GREEK NATIONAL TOURISM ORGANISATION (UK)

5th Floor East, Great Portland House | 4 Great Portland Street, London, W1W 8QJ | tel. 020 7495 9300 | visitgreece. gr

GREEK NATIONAL TOURISM ORGANISATION (USA)

800 Third Avenue, 23rd floor | New York, NY 10022 | tel. 212 421 5777 | visitgreece.gr

GETTING AROUND

BUSES

There are (relatively infrequent) public buses on all the Ionian Islands. The fares are low and tickets are sold by the conductor on board. Timetables are available at bus terminals. They change several times a year depending on the season, and buses run less frequently on Saturdays and Sundays. Also, Greece operates a network of long-distance buses *(Ktel)* which run between the country's cities and islands *(ktelkefalonias.gr, ktel-lefkadas. gr, ktel-zakynthos.gr)*. However, if you are aiming to move around a lot on holiday, it is best not to rely on buses.

DOMESTIC FLIGHTS

Flights in the turbo-prop aircraft of *Sky Express (skyexpress.gr)*, which operates throughout Greece, are very affordable: Aktion (formerly Preveza) to Kefalonia *(around 55 euros)*, Aktion to Zakynthos *(around 60 euros)*, and between Kefalonia and Zakynthos *(around 56 euros)*. Because they fly at low altitudes, these flights are also recommended for day trippers. Kithira, off the south coast of the Peloponnese (historically part of the Ionian Islands) and Corfu, the main island of the archipelago, are also accessible from Zakynthos, Kefalonia and Aktion.

INSIDER TIP Island hopping by plane

FERRIES

Ferries sail from Killini on the Peloponnese (a short trip from Patras) to Zakynthos *(1¼ hrs | approx. 9.50 euros, cars 37 euros | levante ferries.com)*, Poros/Kefalonia *(1½ hrs | approx. 10 euros | levanteferries.com)* and Pisaetos/Ithaca *(2½–3 hrs | approx. 13 euros | levanteferries.com)*. Year-round connections also operate between Nidri/Lefkada, Fiskardo/ Kefalonia and Frikes/Ithaca. Ferries also sail from Astakos on the mainland to Pisoaetos/Ithaca and Sami/ Kefalonia *(ionionpelagos.com)*. We recommend that you book tickets and seats in advance.

HIRE CARS

Mopeds, scooters, motorbikes and cars are available for hire on virtually all the islands, but make sure that you inspect the vehicle carefully beforehand. Many companies offer hire cars; you must be over 21 and have a national driving licence. A small car will cost about 70 euros per week

FESTIVALS & EVENTS
ALL YEAR ROUND

FEBRUARY/MARCH
Carnival Sunday Carnival processions in all of the islands' capitals. The best one is in Zakynthos Town. *greek carnivals.com, zakynthosinformer.com*

APRIL–JUNE
Good Friday Evening processions in all the towns and villages

Easter Saturday Easter mass from 11pm in a sea of candles, plus fireworks

Easter Sunday Private barbecues

Easter Monday Large church festival (*Panigiri*) in Keri on Zakynthos

National holiday The unification of the Ionian Islands with Greece is celebrated in all the capitals with festivals and parades. *21 May*

Pentecost Monday Church festival (*Panigiri*) in Macherado on Zakynthos

JULY/AUGUST
Cultural summer In Argostoli on Kefalonia, with music and theatre performances. *Early July–25 August*

AUGUST
Saristra Festival Palia Vlachata/Sami on Kefalonia, an alternative festival. *Early Aug, saristrafestival.gr*

Largest church festival of the summer In honour of the Virgin Mary; all over, including in Vassiliki on Lefkada and Lixouri on Kefalonia. *15 August*

International Folklore Festival Lefkada Town. *lefkasculturalcenter.gr*

Robola Wine Festival Fragkata/Valsamata, Omala Plateau, Kefalonia, with dancing

Shape Argassi on Zakynthos. Electrohouse festival. *Mid- to end August, shapesfestival.com*

St Dionysios' Festival, patron saint of the Ionian Islands Zakynthos Town, from 7pm procession with fireworks, afterwards festival in the streets and tavernas. *24 August, zakynthos events.com*

AUGUST/SEPTEMBER
Wine festival Zakynthos Town, *wine surveyor.weebly.com*

(hellascar.com) including mileage, full comprehensive cover and tax (excess applies).

Caution: damage to tyres and on the underside of the car is not usually covered by insurance, so be careful: don't drive down any old dirt track!

TAXIS

Taxis are plentiful on all the islands. Only in the larger urban areas, like Zakynthos Town, are they equipped with meters. In all the other cases the driver calculates the price according to the distance. A table showing distances and fares must be visible in every *agoreon* (taxi).

ESSENTIALS

BEACHES

There are many beaches on the islands without lifeguards. Zakynthos has the greatest number of 'managed' beaches. It has a total of 14 Blue Flags, while Kefalonia has 13, and Lefkada has eight. This award, requiring annual renewals, indicates that the beach meets high standards in terms of water quality, safety and environmental management. For an up-to-date map of Blue Flag beaches visit *blueflag.global*.

You should only bathe in the nude on remote beaches, and even if nudist zones are highlighted online, always verify on site that this information is correct. However, topless bathing is acceptable everywhere.

CAMPING

Camping anywhere other than in a campsite is prohibited although people often camp on isolated beaches. Just don't put your tent up in the immediate vicinity of an official campsite! Many of the islands have official campsites that are usually open between May and September. There are campsites on Zakynthos in the island's south and east *(e.g. Camping Zante | Tragaki Beach | tel. 69 77 25 74 93 or Tartaruga Camping | Laganas Bay | tartaruga-camping.com)*; on Kefalonia *(e.g. Camping Argostoli | Fanari near Argostoli | camping-argostoli.gr);* and on Lefkada *(e.g. in Vassiliki | camping vassilikibeach.com or above Kathisma Beach | camping-kathisma.gr).*

CUSTOMS

UK citizens can bring in goods worth up to £390, but there are limits on alcohol and tobacco products, including a 42-litre limit on beer, an 18-litre limit on wine and a 4-litre limit on spirits and liquors. See *gov.uk* for updates.

For EU citizens, the following duty-free allowances apply (import and export): for own consumption 800 cigarettes, 400 cigarillos, 200 cigars, 1kg tobacco, 20 litres of aperitifs, 90 litres of wine (with a maximum of 60 litres for sparkling wine) and 110 litres of beer.

Residents of the US do not have to pay duty on articles purchased overseas up to the value of $800, but there are limits on alcohol and tobacco products. For international travel regulations for US residents please see *cbp.gov*

INTERNET & WIFI

Many hotels and cafés offer free WiFi (which is also referred to as a "hotspot") for guests.

LANGUAGE

The Greeks are proud of their script, which is unique to Greece. Although place names and labels are often also written in Roman letters, it is still useful to have some knowledge of the Greek alphabet – and you really need to know how to stress the words correctly to be understood. It is sometimes the case that the same place name and its surroundings can have three to four different versions of spelling. A touch of imagination is required for finding your way around the islands.

MONEY & PRICES

The currency is the euro and you can withdraw money from many ATMs with your credit or debit card. Often your own bank will charge a fee, depending on the amount, making it cheaper to draw a large amount at once instead of lots of small amounts. *Bank opening hours: Mon–Thu 8am–2pm, Fri 8am–1.30pm.*

Price levels are more or less the same as elsewhere in Europe. Hotel rooms and public transport are cheaper, while petrol and food is more expensive. In general, eating out and visiting a bar are cheaper, but prices will naturally increase in high season.

OPENING HOURS

Shops catering to the tourist trade are open daily 10am–10pm. Supermarkets are usually open Monday to Saturday 8am–9pm. Many non-tourist shops are closed on Monday and Wednesday afternoons. Mini supermarkets are open daily, depending on the season. The majority of restaurants are open daily in high season, with many opening as early as 9am and offering breakfast. Most restaurants are open from lunchtime to midnight. Dance clubs usually only open at around 11pm or midnight. The opening hours specified in this travel guide are subject to frequent changes.

POST

There are post offices in all the towns and on almost all islands; they are mostly open from Monday to Friday 7am–2pm.

PUBLIC HOLIDAYS

1 January	New Year
6 January	Epiphany
February/March	Shrove Monday
25 March	National holiday
April/May	Orthodox Good Friday
April/May	Orthodox Easter
1 May	Labour Day
21 May	Unification of the Ionian Islands
June	Whitsun
15 August	Assumption Day
28 October	National Day (Ochi Day)
25/26 December	Christmas

TELEPHONES & MOBILES

All telephone numbers except for emergency numbers have ten digits. There are no area codes. Mobile numbers are recognisable by their first digit, which is always a "6".

When buying a Greek SIM card to obtain a Greek number, you will always have to present identification. Mobile service providers are Cosmote, Vodafone and Wind.

The dialling code for Greece is *+30*. International dialling codes: UK *+44*, Australia *+61*, Canada *+1*, Ireland *+353* and USA *+1*.

TIPPING

Prices in tavernas include all taxes and official service charges. The bread is accounted for at the end of your meal: if you don't want any bread, please return it immediately. For quenching your thirst, tap water is provided free of charge and is generally brought to you before you order. It is customary to give a 10 to15 per cent tip; chambermaids get 1 euro per room per day; in taxis you can round up the fare by at least 50 cents.

TOILETS

In principle, even in good hotels, you are not allowed to flush toilet paper; put it in the bin provided to avoid clogging up the narrow sewers.

EMERGENCIES

UK EMBASSY

1 Ploutarchou Street | 10675 Athens | tel. 21 07 27 26 00 | gov.uk/world/ organisations/british-embassy-athens

UK CONSULATE

28 Foskolou Street | 29 100 Zakynthos | tel. 26 95 02 29 06 | gov.uk/world/ organisations/british-honorary-vice-consulate-zakynthos

US EMBASSY

91 Vasilissis Sophias Avenue | Athens | tel. 21 07 21 29 51 | gr.usembassy.gov

CANADIAN EMBASSY

48 Ethnikis Antistaseos Street | 15231 Athens | tel. 21 07 27 34 00 | international.gc.ca/coutry-pays/greece-grece/athens-athenes.aspx?lang=eng

EMERGENCY SERVICES

Dial *112* for all the emergency services: police, fire brigade and ambulance. The number is toll free and English is also spoken.

HEALTH

Well-trained doctors guarantee basic medical care on all major islands, but there is sometimes a lack of technical equipment. If you are seriously ill, it is advisable to return home.

UK citizens can theoretically be treated for free by doctors if you present the Global Health Insurance Card (gov.uk/global-health-insurance-card). However, in practice doctors do so reluctantly and it is better to take out private travel insurance that covers medical issues, including repatriation.

There are pharmacies in the larger towns and villages; on the smaller islands, doctors have medication on hand for emergencies.

IMPORTANT NOTES

EARTHQUAKES

Minor earthquakes do occur now and then and are no reason to panic. Should you experience an earthquake, take cover underneath a door lintel, a table or a bed. As soon as the quake is over, you should go outside (do not use the lifts) and then stay clear of walls and flower pots that might fall over. Once outside it is best to follow the lead of the locals.

WEATHER IN ZAKYNTHOS

High season
Low season

	JAN	FEB	MARCH	APRIL	MAY	JUNE	JULY	AUG	SEPT	OCT	NOV	DEC
Daytime temperature	14°	14°	16°	19°	24°	28°	31°	32°	28°	23°	19°	16°
Night-time temperature	5°	5°	7°	9°	12°	16°	18°	18°	16°	13°	10°	7°
Sunshine hours/day	4	5	6	8	10	10	13	11	9	7	5	3
Rainy days/month	13	11	9	7	5	2	1	1	5	9	12	15
Sea temperatures in °C	14°	14°	14°	16°	18°	21°	23°	24°	23°	21°	18°	16°

Sunshine hours/day   Rainy days/month   Sea temperatures in °C

WORDS & PHRASES
IN GREEK

SMALL TALK

Yes/no/maybe	ne/'ochi/'issos	Ναι/ Όχι/Ισως
Please/Thank you	paraka'lo/efcharis'to	Παρακαλώ/ Ευχαριστώ
Good morning/good evening/goodnight!	kalli'mera/kalli'spera/ kalli'nichta!	Καλημέραμ/ Καλησπέρα!/ Καληνύχτα!
Hello/ goodbye (formal)/ goodbye (informal)!	'ya (su/sass)/ a'dio/ ya (su/sass)!	Γεία (σου/σας)!/ αντίο!/Γεία (σου/ σας)!
My name is …	me 'lene …	Με λένεÖ …
What's your name?	poss sass 'lene?	Πως σας λένε?
Excuse me/sorry	me sig'chorite/ sig'nomi	Με συγχωρείτε / Συγνώημ
Pardon?	o'riste?	Ορίστε?
I (don't) like this	Af'to (dhen) mu a'ressi	Αυτό (δεν) ουμ αρέσει

SYMBOLS

EATING & DRINKING

Could you please book a table for tonight for four?	Klis'te mass parakal'lo 'enna tra'pezi ya a'popse ya 'tessera 'atoma	Κλείστε ασμ παρακαλώ ένα τραπέζι γιά απόψε γιά τέσσερα άτοαμ
The menu, please	tonn ka'taloggo parakal'lo	Τον κατάλογο παρακαλώ
Could I please have ... ?	tha 'ithella na 'echo ...?	Θα ήθελα να έχω ...?
more/less	pjo/li'gotäre	ρτιό/λιγότερο
with/without ice/ sparkling	me/cho'ris 'pa-go/ anthrakik'ko	εμ/χωρίς πάγο/ ανθρακικό
(un)safe drinking water	(mi) 'possimo nä'ro	(μη) Πόσιμο νερό
vegetarian/allergy	chorto'fagos/allerg'ia	Χορτοφάγος/ Αλλεργία
May I have the bill, please?	'thel'lo na pli'rosso parakal'lo	Θέλω να πληρώσω παρακαλώ

MISCELLANEOUS

Where is ...?	pu tha vro ...?	Που θα βρω ...?
What time is it?	Ti 'ora 'ine?	Τι ώρα είναι?
How much does... cost ?	Posso 'kani ...?	Πόσο κάνει ...?
Where can I find internet access?	pu bor'ro na vro 'prosvassi sto índernett?	Που πορώμ να βρω πρόσβαση στο ίντερνετ?
pharmacy/ chemist	farma'kio/ ka'tastima	Φαρακείομ/ Κατάστημ καλλυντικών
fever/pain /diarrhoea/ nausea	piret'tos/'ponnos/ dhi'arria/ana'gula	Πυρετός/Πόνος/ Διάρροια/Αναγούλα
Help!/Watch out! Be Careful	Wo'ithia!/Prosso'chi!/ Prosso'chi!	Βοήθεια!/Προσοχή!/ Προσοχή!
Forbidden/banned	apa'goräfsi/ apago'räwäte	Απαγόρευση/ απαγορέυεται
0/1/2/3/4/5/6/7/8/9/ 10/100/1000	mi'dhen / 'enna / 'dhio / 'tria / 'tessera / 'pende /'eksi / ef'ta / och'to / e'nea / dhekka / eka'to / 'chilia / 'dhekka chil'iades	ηδένμ/ένα/δύο/τρία/ τέσσερα/πέντε/έξί/ εφτά/οχτώ/ εννέα/ δέκα/εκατό/χίλια/ δέκα χιλιάδες

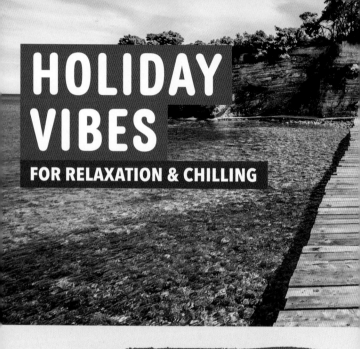

HOLIDAY VIBES
FOR RELAXATION & CHILLING

FOR BOOKWORMS & FILM BUFFS

📖 THE ODYSSEY

Homer's epic is more than 2,700 years old. It is available in several English editions, in both verse and prose form, as well as in a series of audio CDs. *The Odyssey* has also been made into a film many times, including the version by Mario Camerini with Kirk Douglas and Silvana Mangano (1954, two DVDs), and as a TV series with Armand Assante and Greta Scacchi (1997, DVD).

📖 ODYSSEUS & PENELOPE: AN ORDINARY MARRIAGE

An entertaining novel by the classicist Inge Merkel (translated by Renate Latimer) that retells the myth from an unusual perspective.

🎥 CAPTAIN CORELLI'S MANDOLIN

The best-selling novel by Louis de Bernières was also made into a film by John Madden (2001) starring Nicolas Cage and Penelope Cruz. The novel is set in Kefalonia during the World War II.

📖 MAP OF YOU

This novel (2016) by Isabelle Broom is set on Zakynthos and makes for a great summer read. Holly, the heroine, has to discover a family secret on the island, but must also think about her own life. Of course, romance and the beautiful scenery play their part, too...

PLAYLIST

0:58

❙❙ CAPTAIN CORELLI'S MANDOLIN – PELAGIA'S SONG
From the film: Nicolas Cage plays a melody filled with longing.

▶ APOPSE ME TIN KITHARA MOU
A Zakynthian *kantada* that pulls on the heart strings.

▶ NATASSA BOFILIOU – ITHAKI
"I will search for Ithaca," the popular artist sings in this ballad.

▶ GERASIMOS ANDREATOS – CHROMA DEN ALLAZOUNE TA MATIA
The ethno-pop singer with Kefalonian roots has been going since the 1980s.

▶ SAKIS ROUVAS – SHAKE IT
Once a pole vaulter, then he came third in the Eurovision Song Contest 2004 with this song, and now he's a pop star.

The holiday soundtrack can be found on **Spotify** *under* **MARCO POLO** *Greece*

Or scan the code with the Spotify app

ONLINE

ATCORFU.COM
This website doesn't just promote Corfu, but the "cuisine-recipes-and-gastronomy" section provides Ionian recipes for cooking at home.

IZANTE
Free app with information about Zakynthos; can also be used offline.

GREEKA.COM/IONIAN/KEFALONIA/KEFALONIA-VIDEOS-1.HTM
Around 50 videos showing lots of different aspects of Kefalonia.

VISITGREECE.GR/EN/GREEK_ISLANDS/IONIAN_ISLANDS/ZAKYNTHOS
A website with information on the island's history, culture and beaches.

GREEKA.COM/IONIAN/ZAKYNTHOS/ZAKYNTHOS-VIDEOS-1.HTM
A nice selection of around 30 videos in different languages about the island of Zakynthos.

TRAVEL PURSUIT

THE MARCO POLO HOLIDAY QUIZ

Do you know what makes the Ionian Islands tick? Test your knowledge of the idiosyncrasies and eccentricities of these islands and their people. You will find the answers at the bottom of the page and in detail in this guide.

❶ How many islands comprise the Ionian Islands?
a) 4
b) 304
c) 7

❷ Which one was the home of Odysseus?
a) Delphi
b) Ithaca
c) Kefalonia and/or Ithaca

❸ What did the Venetians call Zakynthos during their almost 600-year rule of the Ionian Islands?
a) Fior di Levante
b) Furore des Lavanda
c) Fiore d'acqua

❹ Which was the only island to belong to the Ottoman Empire for two centuries?
a) Corfu
b) Lefkada
c) Meganisi

❺ Which natural resources that are freely accessible on the islands are good for the skin?
a) Slate flakes at the Arethousa well on Ithaca
b) Red clay sand (Xi Beach on Kefalonia) and sulphurous water (Pigadakia, Xigia Beach on Zakynthos)
c) Melting stalactites in the caves of Drogarati and Melissani (Kefalonia)

Beautiful Kioni Bay on Ithaca

❻ What is Zakynthos's best-known landmark?
a) Turtle
b) Shipwreck Beach
c) Kastro in Bochali

❼ Dionysios Solomos, author of the Greek national anthem, was born on which island?
a) Crete
b) Samos
c) Zakynthos

❽ Which animal on the islands is currently threatened by extinction?
a) Mosquito
b) Flamingo
c) Loggerhead turtle

❾ Which goods were smuggled on the *MV Panagiotis*, the ship that ran aground on Shipwreck Beach?
a) Cigarettes
b) Cocaine
c) Diamonds

❿ Which building on the islands is listed in the *Guinness Book of World Records*?
a) Odysseus's palace on Ithaca
b) De Bosset bridge in Argostoli
c) Stonehenge on the mini-golf course in Argassi

INDEX

WE WANT TO HEAR FROM YOU!

Did you have a great holiday? Is there something on your mind? Whatever it is, let us know! Whether you want to praise the guide, alert us to errors or give us a personal tip – MARCO POLO would be pleased to hear from you. Please contact us by email:

We do everything we can to provide the very latest information for your trip. Nevertheless, despite all of our authors' thorough research, errors can creep in. MARCO POLO does not accept any liability for this.

sales@heartwoodpublishing.co.uk

PICTURE CREDITS
Cover photo: Shipwreck Beach (Schapowalow: T. u. B. Morandi)
Photos: Gettyimages: D. Boskovic (95); R. Hackenberg (10, 21); E. Heinze (131); huber-images: R. Schmid (2/3, 85); Laif/Le Figaro Magazine (62/63); Laif/Loop Images: R. Birkby (14/15); Laif/robertharding: (96, 128/129), F. Fell (45); Levante Beer (57); Look/age fotostock (58, 90); Look/TerraVista (72); mauritius images: R. Adler (119), S. Beuthan (33), M. Habel (32/33, 54, 100/101), Miniloc (26/27); mauritius images/age fotostock: J. Wlodarczyk (40/41); mauritius images/Alamy: D. Dimitris (24/25), S. French (86/87), V. Gajic (34/35), C. Iliopoulos (back cover flap, 76, 78/79), D. Kilpatrick (46), M. Longhurst (105), H. Milas (92, 99), J. Morgan (69), D. Tomlinson (83), J. Windsor (115), R. Wyatt (30); mauritius images/Alamy/ funkyfood London: P. Williams (22, 75); mauritius images/foodcollection (28/29, 52); mauritius images/ hemis.fr: R. Mattes (6/7); mauritius images/ib/gourmet-vision (29); mauritius images/Juice Images: I. Lishman (36/37); Shutterstock: Athanasios Giatras (6/7); Adisa (11), Feel good studio (12, 61), kavram (8/9), A. Mayovskyy (126/127), C. Stan (outside front cover, inside front cover/1), P. Stelian (13), I. Tichonow (16/17), G. Tsichlis (66, 70/71), K. Vitaly (48/49), vivooo (51), Zebra-Studio (116/117)

11th Edition - fully revised and updated 2023
Worldwide Distribution: Heartwood Publishing Ltd, Bath, United Kingdom
www.heartwoodpublishing.co.uk

Authors: Klaus Bötig, Elisabeth Heinze
Editor: Manuela Hunfeld, Christin Ullmann
Picture editor: Anja Schlatterer
Cartography: © MAIRDUMONT, Ostfildern (pp. 38–39, 102, 108, 110, 112, 114, pull-out map); © MAIRDUMONT, Ostfildern, using data from OpenStreetMap, licence CC-BY-SA 2.0 (pp. 42–43, 64–65, 80–81, 88–89)
Cover design and pull-out map cover design: bilekjaeger_Kreativagentur with Zukunftswerkstatt, Stuttgart
Page design: Langenstein Communication GmbH, Ludwigsburg

Heartwood Publishing credits:
Translated from the German by Thomas Moser, Robert Scott McInnes; Jozef van der Voort
Editors: Rosamund Sales, Kate Michell, Felicity Laughton, Sophie Blacksell Jones
Prepress: Summerlane Books, Bath
Printed in India

MARCO POLO AUTHOR
ELISABETH HEINZE

In rural Zakynthos you may come across the odd peacock strutting, his feathers on full display. Elisabeth, who travels Greece as a freelance journalist, was immediately gripped by the magic of the Ionian Islands. People here are laid back, unimposing but open-hearted. The opportunity to visit breathtaking locations in absolute tranquility makes for an unforgettable journey for travellers who are open to new experiences.

DOS & DONT'S

HOW TO AVOID SLIP-UPS & BLUNDERS

DON'T ASK ABOUT COMPETITORS
Greeks like to talk to visitors, but don't go into one taverna and ask about another one! You will be told that it doesn't exist, that the owner has passed away or that the police have closed it down. In such a case, you will have to check out the story for yourself.

DO GIVE A TIP
If you are satisfied with the service, tip discreetly. Decide quietly for yourself how much you want to give and simply leave your tip on the table on leaving.

DO CHECK THE PRICE
In restaurants and tavernas, fresh fish is expensive and is often sold by weight. Always ask for the kilo price first, and make sure the fish is weighed in front of you to avoid any unpleasant surprises.

DO KEEP IT COVERED
Greeks are used to seeing some skin in the beach resorts, but in the villages you should dress more conservatively. In the churches and monasteries it is expected that knees and shoulders be covered, and cloaks are often provided at the entrance for hire.

DON'T JUST FOLLOW THE SATNAV
When driving a hire car along breathtaking coastlines, don't just trust your smartphone or satnav, but watch out for road signs and ask local people. Online maps may well send you off on lanes and tracks that only goats can navigate!